THE

CONSTITUTION VIOLATED

AN ESSAY

BY THE AUTHOR OF

THE "MEMOIR OF JOHN GREY OF DILSTON."

DEDICATED TO THE WORKING MEN AND WOMEN OF
GREAT BRITAIN.

EDINBURGH

EDMONSTON AND DOUGLAS

1871.

THE CONSTITUTION VIOLATED.

Edinburgh : Printed by Thomas and Archibald Constable,

FOR

EDMONSTON AND DOUGLAS.

LONDON . . . . HAMILTON, ADAMS, AND CO.

CAMBRIDGE . . . . . MACMILLAN AND CO.

GLASGOW . . . . JAMES MACLEHOSE.

TO MY HUSBAND

AND TO

ANOTHER FRIEND

I OWE A GRATEFUL ACKNOWLEDGMENT OF HELP
GIVEN TO ME IN THE PREPARATION OF THIS LITTLE WORK
DURING SEVERAL WEEKS OF BODILY SUFFERING.

CHAPTER I.

THE object of the following Essay is to set forth the unconstitutional nature of certain recent Acts of the Legislature, and the danger arising therefrom, with the view of arousing the country to a sense of that danger.

The enactments called the Contagious Diseases Acts, passed respectively in 1866, 1868, and 1869, may be regarded from several points of view. With their medical aspect and the statistical consideration of their results on public health, it is not my intention to deal. It has been dwelt on by other people, and in other places, fully.

The moral side of the question is undoubtedly the most important, and has been dwelt upon by the religious portion of the community, almost to the exclusion of others, although it may be truly said that it of necessity includes all others.

There is, however, one aspect of the question which has not been sufficiently set forth, that is, the consti-

tutional aspect, including the effect which such legislation must have on our social and moral life as a
nation, from a political point of view.

In almost all the great meetings which have been
held throughout the country on the subject of these
Acts, resolutions have been passed embodying the word
"unconstitutional" as characteristic of the Acts, proving
that the mass of the people of England have a strong
instinct, if it be nothing more, of what is constitutional
and what is not. Few terms, it has been said, are more
vaguely or loosely employed than this. It is affirmed
with some truth that " Magna Charta is in everybody's
lips but in nobody's hands." The careful study of the
Acts in question leads me to the conclusion that the
latter part of this saying must be eminently true of
their framers. We, on the other hand, are charged by
our opponents with ignorance of the words which we
use. Yet what Sir Edward Creasy says[1] is true, that
" the English Constitution is susceptible of a full and
accurate explanation ;" and though the subject may
require " more investigation than may suit hasty talkers
and superficial thinkers, it is not more than every member of a great and free State ought gladly to bestow, in
order that he may rightly comprehend and appreciate the
polity and the laws in which and by which he lives, acts,

---

[1] *English Constitution*, p. 2. (Eighth edition. Bentley.)

and has his civic being." He adds, "The student will recognise and admire in the history, laws, and institutions of England, certain great leading principles which have existed from the earliest periods of our nationality down to the present time. These great primeval and enduring principles are the principles of the English Constitution; and we are not obliged to learn them from imperfect evidence or precarious speculations, for they are imperishably recorded in the Great Charter, and in the charters and statutes connected with and confirmatory of Magna Carta." It is these enduring principles which are violated by the Contagious Diseases Acts. This I shall shortly show, but before doing so, I shall briefly set forth what these principles are.

I am convinced that the people of this country are as yet but very partially awakened to the tremendous issues involved in the controversy before us, considered as a matter of constitutional rights ; therefore it is that I venture, though I am no lawyer, to bring before them its extreme importance under that aspect. For this time of agony for the patriot, who can in any degree foresee the future of that country which violates the eternal principles of just government, drives many of us, unlearned though we be, to search the annals of our country, to inquire into past crises of danger, and the motives and character of the champions who fought the battles of liberty, with that keenness and singleness of purpose with which, in the agony of spiritual danger, the well-nigh shipwrecked soul may search the Scriptures of God, believing that in them he has eternal life.

On the occasion of an infringement of a constitutional principle by Parliament itself, a century ago, Lord Chatham, when urging the House of Lords to retrace this fatal step, used the following words :—"If I had a doubt upon this matter, I should follow the example set us by the most reverend bench, with whom I believe it is a maxim, when any doubt in point of faith arises, or any question of controversy is started, to appeal at once to the greatest source and evidence of our religion—I mean the Holy Bible. The Constitution has its political Bible also, by which, if it be fairly consulted, every political question may and ought to be determined. Magna Charta, the Petition of Rights, and the Bill of Rights, form that code which I call the Bible of the English Constitution."[1]

In following out this advice of Lord Chatham, it is to these authorities that I wish to appeal in determining the exact nature of those principles of the Constitution which I assert have been violated. I am aware that in doing so I may incur criticism on account

[1] Speech of the Earl of Chatham on the exercise of the Judicature in matters of Election, 1763.

of my ignorance of legal terms and definitions, and on account of unskilfulness in the arrangement of the matter before me. I shall be satisfied, however, if I succeed in commending my subject to those to whom I particularly address myself—I mean the working men and working women of England. Neither they nor I have had a legal training, but we may alike possess a measure of that plain English common sense which, to quote again Lord Chatham's words, is " the foundation of all our English jurisprudence,"—which common sense tells us that " no court of justice can have a power inconsistent with, or paramount to, the known laws of the land, and that the people, when they choose their representatives, never mean to convey to them a power of invading the rights or trampling upon the liberties of those whom they represent."[1] Further on in this Essay I shall show that Parliament in making the Contagious Diseases Acts, has invaded and trampled on the liberties of the people.

I feel sure that those to whom I address myself will, with me, respond readily to this wholesome maxim, that " in every question in which my liberty or my property are concerned, I would consult and be determined by the dictates of common sense." " I confess," continues Lord Chatham, " that I am apt to dis-

[1] Lord Chatham's Speeches.

trust the refinements of learning, because I have seen the ablest and most learned men equally liable to deceive themselves, and to mislead others. The condition of human nature would be lamentable indeed if nothing less than the greatest learning and talents which fall to the share of so small a number of men were sufficient to direct our judgment and conduct. But Providence has taken better care of our happiness, and given us, in the simplicity of common sense, a rule for our direction by which we shall never be misled. . . . The evidence which truth carries with it is superior to all argument ; it neither wants the support nor dreads the opposition of the greatest abilities." And to evince this truth of which I speak, I have preferred to go to the original sources ; and in cases where my own words would have little or no weight, I shall give frequently and copiously the words of our great constitutional writers,—men, the exercise of whose learning and abilities was guided and directed by that plain common sense and reverential regard of principles which are the only safe guides in legislation. I shall make no apology for an occasional lengthy quotation, because although the books from which I quote are or may be in the hands of all persons of the more privileged classes, I am aware that the working classes have little time or opportunity for consulting them.

Among the clauses in Magna Charta, there is one upon which the importance of all the others hinges, and upon which the security afforded by the others practically depends. This clause, and the supplementary clause which follows it, have been those whose subject has formed, more than any other, matter and occasion for the great battles fought for English liberty and right since the Charter was signed by King John.

They are the 39th and 40th clauses of King John's Charter, and the 29th of that of King Henry III., and are as follows :—

39. Nullus liber homo capiatur, vel imprisonetur, aut utlagetur, aut exuletur, aut aliquo modo destruatur, nec super eum ibimus, nec super eum mittemus, nisi per legale judicium parium suorum, vel per legem terræ. 40. Nulli vendemus, nulli negabimus, aut differemus rectum aut justitiam.

39. NO FREEMAN SHALL BE TAKEN, OR IMPRISONED, OR DISSEISED, OR OUTLAWED, OR BANISHED, OR ANYWAYS DESTROYED, NOR WILL WE PASS UPON HIM, NOR WILL WE SEND UPON HIM, UNLESS BY THE LAWFUL JUDGMENT OF HIS PEERS, OR BY THE LAW OF THE LAND. 40. WE WILL SELL TO NO MAN, WE WILL NOT DENY TO ANY MAN EITHER JUSTICE OR RIGHT.

" These clauses are the crowning glories of the great

charter."[1] Mr. Hallam calls them its "essential clauses,"[2]
being those which "protect the personal liberty and
property of all freemen, by giving security from arbitrary imprisonment and spoliation."[3] The same high
authority observes that these words of the Great
Charter, "interpreted by any honest court of law,
convey an ample security for the two main rights of
civil society." The principles of this clause of the
Great Charter, which, if we look backwards, are lost in
antiquity, were subsequently confirmed and elucidated
by statutes and charters of the reign of Henry III. and
Edward III. entitled "confirmationes cartarum." "The
famous writ of Habeas Corpus was framed in conformity
with the spirit of this clause ; that writ, rendered more
actively remedial by the statute of Charles II., but
founded upon the broad basis of Magna Charta, is the
principal bulwark of English liberty, and if ever temporary circumstances, or the doubtful plea of necessity,
shall lead men to look on its denial with apathy, the
most distinguishing characteristic of our constitution
will be effaced."[4]

De Lolme[5] speaks thus of these famous clauses,
articles, or chapters : "They insured that no subject

---

[1] *English Constitution*, p. 148.
[2] *Middle Ages*, chap. ii. p. 324.   [3] *Ibid.*   [4] *Ibid.*
[5] De Lolme on the Constitution, p. 28.

should ever, in any shape whatever, be molested in person or effects otherwise than by the judgment of his peers, and according to the law of the land; an article. so important that it may be said to comprehend the whole end and design of political societies." The same powerful testimony is given by Guizot and De Tocqueville.

It is precisely these very clauses, thus endearingly eulogized by these great historians and lawyers of various nations, which stand violated both in letter and in principle by the Contagious Diseases Acts.

Lord Coke[1] speaks thus of these clauses : " These are all words which should be carefully read over and over again, for as the gold-finer will not out of the dust, shreds, or shreds of gold let passe the least crum in respect of the excellency of the metal, so ought not the learned reader to passe any syllable of this law, in respect of the excellency of the matter." " As to the extent of the applicability of the words of the charter," Sir Edward Creasy says,[2] " it is not a piece of class legislation, but its benefits apply to all the freemen of the land, and all freemen are equal in the eye of this great law." Lord Chatham speaks thus of the temper in which this great article of the charter was contended for by the Barons : " They did not confine it to them-

---

[1] Coke on Magna Charta.   [2] *English Constitution*, p. 150.

selves alone, but delivered it as a common blessing to the whole people; they did not say, these are the rights of the great Barons, or these are the rights of the great Prelates; no, but they said, in the simple Latin of the times, 'Nullus liber Homo,' and provided as carefully for the meanest subject as for the greatest. These are uncouth words, and sound but poorly in the ears of scholars, neither are they addressed to the criticism of scholars, but to the hearts of free men. These three words, 'Nullus liber Homo,' have a meaning which interests us all; they deserve to be remembered, they deserve to be inculcated on our minds, they are worth all the classics." The words " Nullus liber Homo" did not originally apply to every person living in England, because a portion of the population was in a state of serfdom or villeinage, which was in effect slavery. But this slavery was in the course of time abolished, and the seeds of enfranchisement were sown by the Great Charter itself. "For[1] through the action of its principles, the villeins (or slaves) were constantly rising into freemen, so that the ultimate effect of this clause was to give and to guarantee full protection for person and property to every human being who breathes English air." In a future portion of this Essay it will be shown how by the enactments which we deplore a por-

[1] *English Constitution*, p. 151.

tion of the community is continually passing from the
state of freemen into the state of slavery, and is in effect
by the action of the Contagious Diseases Acts put, with
respect to the operation of the law, out of the pale of
those denominated by the words "liber Homo."

The universal opinion of lawyers and statesmen
among ourselves, that these clauses of Magna Charta
are the most important bulwark of our liberties, is confirmed by the opinion of a celebrated foreign writer,[1]
who concludes a great work on the penal process of
England, Scotland, and the United States with these
words : "It will be more and more acknowledged how
true it is that the penal legislation of a nation is the
keystone of that nation's public law." Another great
writer on Laws says :[2] "It is upon the excellence of
the criminal laws that chiefly the liberty of the citizen
depends ;" and these words, "the liberty of the citizen,"
what do they not include? Of the same nature are
the weighty words of Lieber[3] on "the value of a well-
guarded penal trial as an element of constitutional
liberty." Sir Edward Creasy, in his sketch of the
general administration of justice in England, begins
with "the criminal law as first in constitutional importance."[4]   I might multiply quotations from great

1 Mittermaier.   2 Montesquieu, *Esprit des Lois*, xii. 2.
3 *Civil Liberty and Self-Government*, p. 54.
4 *English Constitution*, p. 382.

lawyers, showing an universal concurrence in the opinion that without justice in our criminal code we cannot possess that freedom which is one of the conditions of virtue in a nation.

It is not requisite for my purpose to enter into a critical examination of each of the words and phrases of the great clause of Magna Charta referred to, nor even to quote a selection of comments on these words and phrases from the voluminous writings which exist on the subject. There are two expressions, however, as to the meaning of which I shall make a few remarks. The first, as bearing more particularly on the subject in hand, viz., the phrase " aut aliquo modo destruatur;" and the second, the words " per legem terræ," in order that I may with respect to these words correct a misunderstanding which may arise in the mind of a reader who reads them without the light of those subsequent comments and charters which have elucidated Magna Charta.

As to the phrase " aut aliquo modo destruatur" (nor be in any way destroyed), Blackstone, as well as other writers, gives a very wide signification to this word "destroy;" and, in general terms, it may be said that they agree in understanding that these words of the charter sternly forbid any proceeding on the body of an accused person unless after trial by jury. If it were possible for me here to describe in detail that proceeding which the Acts in question sanction upon the body of a person suspected or accused, and who has been condemned without any jury trial, no further words of mine would be needed to convince my readers that this proceeding comes within the scope of that word "destroy." Since, however, the subject is one of which we are not permitted to speak, as society in its present state seems to judge an indecent action to be less reprehensible than the plain words which would be needful to bring that indecent action to light and to judgment, I refrain from doing more here than asserting, and I do assert in the strongest manner, that the compulsory proceedings upon the unwilling bodies of the subjects of these Acts are in the strictest sense of the term a "destruction," as indicated in the words of Magna Charta, and elucidated by subsequent comments and events. The hardest part of this whole controversy is, that the deepest wrong among all these wrongs is unmentionable.

Amongst many curious instances in the history of England of the jealous spirit in which the slightest bodily injury which had been inflicted without a jury trial was resented by the people of England, I will merely quote one, the case of Sir John Coventry :—

Sir John Coventry had animadverted upon some of the King's immoralities. The King (Charles II.) declared that if he did not punish this it would grow a fashion to talk so, and sent some of his guards to watch in the streets where Sir John lodged, and to leave some mark upon his person which should teach him not to talk at that rate for the future. The rest I give in the quaint words of Bishop Burnet:[1] " Sands and Obrian and some others went thither, and as Coventry was going home they drew about him. He stood up to the wall, and snatched the flambeau out of his servant's hand, and with that in the one hand and his sword in the other he defended himself so well that he got more credit by it than by all the actions of his life. He wounded some of them, but they cut his nose to the bone, to teach him to remember what respect he owed to the King; and so they left him, and went back to the Duke of Monmouth's, where Obrian's arm was dressed. That matter was executed by orders from the Duke of Monmouth, for which he was severely censured, because he lived there in professions of friendship with Coventry. Coventry had his nose so well needled up that the scar was scarce ever to be discovered. This put the House of Commons in a furious uproar; they passed a bill of banishment against the actors of it, and put a clause in it that it should not be in the King's power to pardon them."

[1] *History of his Own Times.*

De Lolme quotes this as an instance of the habit of the English people of falling back upon their ancient constitutional rights, remarking that in this instance, although the nose in question was so skilfully needled up as to be as good as ever, still it was deemed by Parliament that the clause "nor in any ways destroyed" of Magna Charta had been violated by this assault, and adds that the whole of Parliament was thrown into such a passion of fury on the occasion that nothing would serve them but the passing of the Act which stands upon the statute-books till this day as the Coventry Act.

If I dared to bring before my readers the comparison of this slight personal insult offered to one man on one occasion, with those day by day perpetrated under the Acts which we oppose, whose effects are to degrade and harden, the nation would not rest content with repeal, but would require an Act to be framed which would render such outrages impossible in the future.[1]

Without needlessly multiplying quotations from our great constitutional writers, it is impossible to convey

---

[1] Sir Charles Trevelyan, in *Good Words* of January 1, 1871, says —" It is well that the ladies of England have protested against their sex being recognised by Parliament as a *corpus vile* for the indulgence of irregular lust. If it were possible for them to explain the real extent of the outrage upon womanhood, there would be one universal cry for repeal throughout the land."

to my readers an adequate notion of the strictness of meaning of the one expression in Magna Charta, "We will destroy no one unless by the judgment of his peers." It is by the great lawyers interpreted to mean, that no proceeding of any kind whatever of a compulsory nature shall be permitted on the person of any one except after jury trial. Blackstone and others, to make the matter more plain, minutely define those cases in which alone this prohibition of Magna Charta may be set aside, viz., in the punishment of young children by their parents, and of pupils by their masters, but even these were to be kept within the bounds of decency and humanity. I will only quote the words of De Lolme[1] on this subject: "Thus it was made one of the articles of Magna Charta, that the executive power should *not touch the person of the subject*, but in consequence of a judgment passed upon him by his peers; and so great was afterwards the general union in maintaining this law, that the trial by jury which so effectually secures the subject against all the attempts of power, even against such as may be made under the sanction of the judicial authority, hath been preserved till this day."

In the clause of Magna Charta upon which we have dwelt, the words " per legem terræ" (by the law of the

---

[1] De Lolme on the Constitution, p. 354.

land) occur. It might be supposed by a rude observer
that these words were meant to refer to something
other than jury trial, and might perhaps include such
Acts of Parliament as those which we reprobate. The
various clauses of Magna Charta have been elucidated
and confirmed no less by subsequent enactments than
by famous State trials, which have led to clear definitions of what is to be understood by each clause.
Among the clauses thus confirmed and elucidated, there
has been none more dwelt upon than that "per legem
terræ," the contentions over which single expression
have served again and again to confirm and securely
establish the liberties of England. It is in the light of
these subsequent confirmations and elucidations that
great lawyers are enabled to read the words of Magna
Charta with a certainty which could never have otherwise been attached to them, and to give to every word
of that charter a fulness of meaning which cannot be
gathered from a study of the text alone.

The words "per legem terræ" have been taken by some
not to refer to jury trial. Attempts have been made
to justify illegal proceedings by this interpretation.
This has given rise to arguments and enactments, by
means of which the relation of these words to jury
trial has been settled beyond dispute; and it is these
arguments and enactments which as much as anything

else have thrown light on the ancient institution of
jury trial, and have confirmed as a lasting and inalien-
able part of the Constitution, this ancient " law of the
land." One of the most marked discussions on this
subject, ending with the establishment of the principle
which we have laid down, that jury trial is the one
constitutional form of trial recognised in Magna Charta,
took place in the reign of Charles I., when Judge Selden,
at the time of the arrest of the five members, made a
famous speech, pleading for the release of Sir E. Hampden
from illegal imprisonment, on the ground that these
words "per legem terræ," showed that it was illegal to imprison him by any other method than that of jury trial.

There were also several Statutes passed in the reign
of Edward II. and III., distinctly interpreting these words
to mean, by the old law of England, viz., by jury trial.[1]

I refer to these arguments regarding this expression
" per legem terræ," not, as will be evident to my readers,

[1] See Coke, p. 50, on Magna Charta. He says, "Nisi per legem
terræ," but by the law of the land. For the true sense and exposi-
tion of these words see the Statute of 37 Edward III. cap. 8, where
the words ' but by the law of the land' are rendered ' without
due process of law ;' for there it is said, though it be contained in the great charter that no man is to be taken, imprisoned,
or put out of his freehold without process of law, that is, without
indictment or presentment 'of good and lawful men, where such
deeds be done in due manner, or by writ original of common law,"
etc. In 28 Edward III. ch. 3, the words are rendered "without
being brought in to answer but by due process of the common law."

because of the insufficiency of the words which precede them, " the judgment of his peers," which in themselves are sufficient to establish and guard the principle of jury trial, but because of the danger which has arisen, and might arise again, of the attempt to substitute in place of jury trial a modern enactment calling itself the law of the land.

And if one thing more than another were required to confirm the assertion that Acts of Parliament, which are destructive of jury trial, are by no means included in the words " per legem terræ," we find that confirmation in a passage by Lord Coke, which not only substantiates what I have said, but also strongly, and almost prophetically, confirms the soundness of the grounds of our opposition to the particular Acts in question.

In commenting on the words " per legem terræ " he says :[1] " Against this ancient and fundamental law," [meaning thereby the " lex terræ" referred to in Magna Charta,] " and in the face thereof, I find an Act of Parliament (11 Hy. VII. cap. 3) made, that as well justices of assize as justices of peace (without any finding of or presentment of the verdict of twelve men), upon a bare information for the king before them made, should have full power and authority by their discretions to mark and determine all offences and contempts committed or

---

[1] Coke's *Institutes*, p. 50.

done by any person or persons against the form, ordinance, and effect of any statute made and not repealed, etc. . . . . By colour of which Act, shaking this fundamental law, it is not credible what horrible oppressions and exactions to the undoing of infinite numbers of people were committed by Sir Richard Empson, Knt., and Edm. Dudley, being justices of peace, throughout England, and upon this unjust and injurious act (as commonly in like cases it falleth out[1]) a new office was created, and they made masters of the king's forfeitures. But at the parliament holden in the first year of Henry VIII., this Act of Henry VII. is recited and made void and repealed, and the reason thereof is yielded (Hy. VIII. cap. 6), for that by force of the said Act it was manifestly known that many sinister and crafty, feigned, and forged informations had been pursued against divers of the king's subjects to their great damage and wrongful vexation. And the ill success thereof, and the fearful ends of these two oppressors, should deter others from committing the like, and should admonish parliaments that, instead of this ordinary and precious trial 'per legem terræ,' they bring not in absolute and partial trials by discretion."

[1] From this we may expect, following out the Contagious Diseases Acts, that a new office under Government will be created analogous to the Bureau de Mœurs in Paris, and that we shall ere long have a Secretary of State for the regulation of vice.

CHAPTER II.

I HAVE now set forth the great principles of Magna Charta, and the foundations of these principles, and have endeavoured to show how much English liberty depends on the preservation of jury trial. I have now to show how the Contagious Diseases Acts destroy these bulwarks of English liberty.

Before doing this, however, it is well to dispose of one vague objection, which may exist in some people's minds, to arguments against these Acts based on the universality of civil rights. There is abroad in many men's minds a vague sort of notion that these Acts in question as they stand on the statute-book of England apply to the army and navy. We cannot perhaps wonder at this mistake—although it is an extraordinary mistake—existing more or less in the minds of the partially informed, when we find that the Member for a learned University, who last session led the opposition in the House to Mr. Fowler's motion for the repeal of the Acts, based his arguments for the existence of these Acts on the State necessity of having a standing army!

Such statements as these are calculated to lead the public to imagine that these Acts have at least some connection, more or less remote, with the army and navy, and in this way to allay those just alarms which must necessarily arise from the violation of the constitutional rights of civilians.

Now the fact is, that so far from these Acts applying particularly to the army and navy, they in no way whatsoever apply to the army and navy, but entirely and exclusively to the civil population. The one and only connection which they have with the army and navy is, that the districts to which they apply are those within at least ten miles of which soldiers or sailors are resident. But in these districts they apply not to soldiers or sailors, but to the civil population, and to the civil population only. The word soldier or sailor does not occur in the whole Act, nor is there anything whatsoever about the army or navy, or any hint, the most remote, of any connection with the army or navy, except this, that the whole powers of carrying out the Acts are intrusted to the Admiralty and War Office. In fact, the jurisdiction of these offices is by these Acts extended over a large portion of the civil population of England. Nay, so little has the Act to do with soldiers and sailors, that it does not even commence with the preamble which, unless it had distinctly acknowledged its necessary separation from the army and navy, we should have expected to find in some such words as these, " Considering the increase of contagious disease in her Majesty's army and navy," and so forth. Over and above the obvious fact, that women, to whom alone the Act applies, are in no case members of these honourable services, the Acts do not even profess in any way whatsoever to apply particularly to those women who associate with soldiers and sailors, but distinctly leave us to infer the opposite; for in clause 4, Act 1869, directions are given for procedure against any woman whom the policeman believes to have been, under certain circumstances, in the company of *men* resident within the limits to which the Act applies, the word " men " being used with no reference to soldiers or sailors at all. In fact, the idea that the Acts apply in any way to the army or navy is so absolutely unfounded, that a confutation of it seems almost absurd, and I would not have mentioned it but for the fallacious notion on this point promoted apparently by the supporters of the Acts, encouraged by such statements as that of Dr. Lyon Playfair, already referred to, and confirmed by the natural practice of most persons of taking their information as to an Act of Parliament at second hand. In passing I would, however, point it out as a very grave objection to these Acts, that they extend the jurisdiction of the Admiralty and War Office over the civil population, and that they intrust to these offices such extensive and arbitrary powers as we shall shortly see that they do.[1]

The Contagious Diseases Acts, as now in force, consist essentially of the following clauses :—

Act 1869, Clause 4.—" Where an information on oath is laid before a justice by a superintendent of police[2]

---

[1] "Touching the business of martial law, these things are to be observed, viz.—*First*, that in truth and reality it is not a law, but something indulged rather than allowed as a law. The necessity of government, order, and discipline in an army, is that only which can give those laws a continuance : 'quod enim necessitas cogit defendit.' *Secondly*, This indulged law was only to extend to members of the army, and never was so much indulged as intended to be executed or exercised upon others. For others who are not listed under the army had no colour or reason to be bound by military constitutions applicable only to the army, whereof they were not parts. But they were to be ordered and governed only according to the laws to which they were subject."—Hale's *Common Law of England*, vol. i. p. 54.

"The Admiralty Court is not bottomed or founded upon the authority of the civil law, but hath its power and jurisdiction in such matters as are proper for its cognizance. The Court of Admiralty has no jurisdiction of matters or contracts done or made on land ; and the true reason for their jurisdiction in matters done at sea is because no jury can come from thence."—*Ibid.* p. 51.

[2] Under Act 1866 the police are defined to mean " Metropolitan police, or other police or constabulary authorized to act in any part of any place to which this Act applies."

Act 1868 was especially passed for the sole reason of substituting in Ireland "any policeman duly authorized," instead of "the superintendent of police."

charging to the effect that the informant has good cause
to believe that a woman, therein named, is a common
prostitute, and either is resident within the limits of
any place to which this Act applies, or, being resident
within ten miles of these limits, or, having no settled
place of abode, has within fourteen days before the lay-
ing of the information either been within those limits
for the purpose of prostitution, or been outside of those
limits for the purpose of prostitution in the company of
men resident within those limits, the justice may, if
he thinks fit, issue a notice thereof addressed to such
woman, which notice the superintendent of police shall
cause to be served on her."

Act 1866, Clause 16.—"In either of the following
cases, namely,"—

" If the woman on whom such a notice is served
appears herself, or by some person on her behalf, at the
time and place appointed in the notice, or at some
other time and place appointed by adjournment;"—

"If she does not so appear, and it is shown (on oath)
to the justice present that the notice was served on her
a reasonable time before the time appointed for her
appearance, or that reasonable notice of such adjournment was given to her (as the case may be);"—

" The justice present, on oath being made before him
substantiating the matter of the information to his

satisfaction, may, if he thinks fit, order that the woman be subject to a periodical medical examination by the visiting surgeon for any period not exceeding one year, for the purpose of ascertaining at the time of each such examination whether she is affected with a contagious disease; and thereupon she shall be subject to such a periodical medical examination, and the order shall be a sufficient warrant for the visiting surgeon to conduct such examination accordingly."

We who have combined to oppose this legislation maintain that this Act is unconstitutional, because it submits a case, in which the result is to the party concerned of the most enormous consequence, to trial without jury.

We are well aware, while making this statement, that there is a class of cases in England which at this present time are tried without a jury. But these cases are what are called " minor cases."

Now we maintain that a woman's honour is a point of very grave importance to her, and that no State can thrive in which ·it is not regarded as a very sacred question. And we maintain that a case which is to decide as to the question of a woman's honour is by no means, nor by any stretch of language or imagination, capable of being called a " minor case."

We therefore maintain that this law, which places the determination of the fact as to a woman's honour

solely in the hands of a single justice of the peace, is as
great an infringement of constitutional right, as if the
determination of the fact as to whether a man were
guilty of murder or not were placed in the hands of a
single justice of the peace.

We maintain absolutely that to deprive of jury trial
a woman whose honour is the subject in question, is a
breach of the English Constitution, as fundamentally
expressed in that clause of Magna Charta of which we
have already pointed out the importance, "We will
condemn no one except by the judgment of his peers."

The decision of the question as to her honour would
itself, even if followed by no legal consequences, be a
sufficiently grave one to warrant what I say. But let
it be observed that when the case is decided against the
woman, the deprivation of her honour is followed
immediately, under these Acts, by those consequences
which are especially indicated in Magna Charta as the
consequences which shall ensue to no one except after
trial by jury. She is not only subjected to that ordeal
which we assert comes distinctly within the application
of the words " or anyways destroyed;" but in order to
the carrying out of that ordeal, she is, by the Act,
both outlawed and imprisoned in the strict meaning of
these terms as used in Magna Charta. She is in fact
deprived of her liberties for the space of a year. She

is outlawed practically during that period, inasmuch
as she is handed over to the irresponsible action of
surgeons, at whose simple fiat she may be detained
and imprisoned without even any order before a
justice, or any oath or affidavit taken.[1] Her whole
liberty is curtailed, inasmuch as she is liable to
be summoned for a repetition of this ordeal at whatever times and as frequently as the surgeon thinks
fit; and the entire curtailment which this is of her
liberty must be evident from the fact that she is bound
to appear, subject to the penalty of imprisonment, with
or without hard labour.   I have already said that

---

[1] 20. If in any such examination the woman examined is found to
be affected with a contagious disease, she shall thereupon be liable
to be detained in a certified hospital, subject and according to the
provisions of this Act, and the visiting surgeon shall sign a certificate to the effect that she is affected with a contagious disease,
naming the certified hospital in which she is to be placed, and he
shall sign that certificate in triplicate, and shall cause one of the
originals to be delivered to the woman, and the others to the
superintendent of police.

21. Any woman to whom any such certificate of the visiting
surgeon relates may, if she thinks fit, proceed to the certified hospital named in that certificate, and place herself there for medical
treatment; but if, after the certificate is delivered to her, she
neglects or refuses to do so, the superintendent of police, or a constable acting under his orders, shall apprehend her and convey her
with all practicable speed to that hospital, and place her there for
medical treatment, and the certificate of the visiting surgeon shall
be sufficient authority to him for so doing.

22. Where a woman certified by the visiting surgeon to be
affected with a contagious disease places herself, or is placed as
aforesaid, in a certified hospital for medical treatment, she shall be

these Acts virtually introduce a species of villeinage or slavery. I use the word not sentimentally, but in the strictest legal sense. Slavery means that condition in which an individual is not master of his own person, and the condition of slavery is defined in Magna Charta by the omission of all slaves from the rights which that charter grants to every one else. There could be no more complete, galling, and oppressive deprivation of freedom than this which takes place under these Acts. Nor is this compulsory attendance and detention wherever and whenever a surgeon may please the only loss of freedom to which the woman is subject, and which strictly comes under the meaning of the words of Magna Charta, "We will imprison no one;" but she is liable further by the clauses of the Act already quoted in the note to be detained in an hospital for a period so long as nine months, which is distinctly

detained there for that purpose by the chief medical officer of the hospital until discharged by him by writing under his hand.

The certificate of the visiting surgeon, one of the three originals whereof shall be delivered by the superintendent of police to the chief medical officer, shall, when so delivered, notwithstanding that she is for that purpose removed out of one into or through another jurisdiction, or is detained in a jurisdiction other than that in which the certificate of the visiting surgeon was made, shall be sufficient authority for such detention.

26. Every woman conveyed or transferred under this Act to a certified hospital, shall, while being so conveyed or transferred thither, and also while detained there, be deemed to be legally in the custody of the person conveying, transferring, or detaining her.

defined under the Acts (see clause 26) as an imprisonment, and is such that she may (see clause 28, quoted
below), if she quits it without being discharged by
the surgeon, be " taken into custody, without warrant,
by any constable." These are obvious contraventions
of the chapter of Magna Charta referred to, and no
argument is required to establish that they are such.
It is not however out of place to show here an additional consequence which follows directly on a woman's
being registered as a "public woman," and which is by no
means the least of the evils which accrue to her under
this Act. Indeed, if we consider it rightly, it is virtually that which comprehends all the rest. According
to Magna Charta it is not only a subject's person and
liberty which shall be untouched, except after trial by
jury, but also his property. Now the honour of a poor
woman is often her only capital ; it is in fact that part
of her property the loss of which is ruin to her ; the
action of this law therefore, by registering a woman as
infamous, deprives her of that character the possession
of which is, in almost every case, her only hope of
getting a living in an honest situation, and the loss of
which, whether it be lost rightly or wrongly, is ruinous
to her whole future life.

Now here let me once more quote the clause of Magna
Charta, and let the reader place for himself these abomi-

nable Acts in the full light which is flashed upon them
by that sun which enlightens English liberty :—

"No freeman shall be taken, or imprisoned, or disseised, or outlawed, or banished, or anyways destroyed,
nor will we pass upon him, nor will we send upon him,
unless by the lawful judgment of his peers, or by the
law of the land. We will sell to no man, we will not
deny to any man either justice or right."

I am perfectly aware that the absolute letter of
this law has been for a period of years set aside in
what are called "minor cases." With the propriety of
thus infringing on Magna Charta, even in respect to
these minor cases, many great lawyers have had grave
doubts, and have strongly expressed an opinion that
these cases should not be multiplied or extended. Into
this question of minor cases I shall enter more fully in
a subsequent chapter ; but this case is one of an utterly
different nature, involving both the determination of
a grave question and the infliction of a grave and pro-
longed penalty.

It is quite possible for a law to be contrary to law. I
maintain that this law is contrary to law when judged by
the higher laws of the Constitution, to which every law
in England is as amenable, and by which it may be as
distinctly put on its trial, as we who live in England are
amenable to, and may be tried by, the laws of the land.

"There are," says Chancellor Fortescue,[1] "laws made
which may better deserve to be called corruptions than
laws." We maintain that this law is a corruption,
and we unhesitatingly call on all men and women in
England to unite in putting it down; in doing which
we have a very great cause to contend for—the cause
of the liberties of England, concerning which I will
quote what Blackstone says. "It is therefore,"[1] says
he, speaking of trial by jury, "upon the whole a
duty which every man owes to his country, his friends,
his posterity, and himself, to maintain to the utmost
of his power this valuable constitution in all its rights,
to restore it to its ancient dignity, if at all impaired
by the different value of property, or otherwise deviated
from its first institution, to amend it wherever it is
defective; and, above all, to guard with the most jealous
circumspection against the introduction of new and
arbitrary methods of trial, which, under a variety of
plausible pretences, may in time imperceptibly undermine this best preservative of English liberty."

In answer to our objections to these Acts, it is utter
vanity and folly in any one to plead that they apply
only to women who are prostitutes. Can it be supposed
that there is any man in England so foolish as to think
that the safeguards of English law exist for the sake of

[1] *De laudibus legum Angliæ*, p. 53.   [2] Blackstone, Bk. iii. p. 38.

the guilty only ? They exist for the sake of the innocent, who may be falsely accused, as well to protect
them when accused, as to lessen. the chances of unjust
accusation. And can it be supposed that we are so
blind as ever to be able to fancy that it is impossible
that under this law an innocent woman may be accused ? On the contrary, it is obvious that the question of a woman's honour is one in which mistaken
accusations are peculiarly likely to occur. Hence it
has been that in Christian countries the sin of unchastity in a woman has ceased to be treated as legally
criminal, on account, first, of the extreme facility of
false accusation ; and, second, of the impossibility of
rebutting such accusation ; and in more enlightened
communities the injustice has been apparent of treating
penally this offence in one sex only. Yet here we see
a law which, regardless of these considerations, not only
takes in hand the determination as to the question of a
woman's honour, but in the process of that determination deprives her of the only legal safeguard which it
bestows in all other cases. We ought never to forget
that the very fact of jury trial, which guards the person
wrongfully accused, does itself also, more than any other
thing, prevent such wrong accusations. Nor is there
any accusation so likely to be multiplied by the absence
of trial by jury as that against a woman's honour.

C

In presence of this enormity of these Acts, it is perhaps almost trivial to indicate a minor point in which they are unjust. It will be satisfactory to do so, however, in order to show the spirit of utter contempt for woman's honour which this law evinces. The Acts require no witness against the woman except the policeman, who, though he must substantiate on oath his own belief that the woman is a prostitute, is not bound to produce on oath what the grounds of that belief are.[1] If the justice of peace is satisfied with this substantiation, the woman is condemned under the Act.

The honour therefore of every woman is by this law intrusted to two men, the one the justice of the peace, and the other the policeman, who, let it be carefully observed, is expressly hired by Government for the one stated object of detecting unchaste women.

"Every new tribunal," says Blackstone,[2] " erected for the decision of facts without the intervention of a jury (whether composed of justices of the peace, commissioners of the revenue, judges of a court of con-

---

[1] The Act upon this point was very clearly defined by Mr. Bennett, an eminent solicitor, in a case tried at the Duke of Cornwall Hotel, Plymouth, which entirely turned on the fact that *suspicion* alone in the policeman's mind justified his action, and that, further, he was not bound, when called on, to give the reasons of this suspicion.

[2] Blackstone, Book iii.

science, or any other standing magistrates), is a step towards establishing aristocracy, the most oppressive of absolute governments." We are very near being threatened by this absolutism which Blackstone dreads, when we find that this newly erected tribunal is placed under the control of the least responsible, most arbitrary, and most aristocratic portion of all the public offices, and which have ere this been made the tool of dangerous attacks on English liberty.

In answer to all this argument we shall be undoubtedly met with the assurance that the decisions of this tribunal will seldom err, because honourable and upright men will be employed; that the case is always one of such perfect clearness, that it needs only ordinary judgment and care to decide it, and that the chances of false accusation are thus reduced to a minimum.[1]

Concerning this argument, it is well to relate that a gentleman once, who despised what in his estimation were unnecessary precisenesses of mathematics, on being asked to find the centre of a circle, after having inspected

[1] M. Le Cour says that in Paris false accusations, by anonymous letters and otherwise, amount to several hundreds a week.

In the case at Plymouth already alluded to, Inspector Annis of Plymouth being asked by Mr. Rooker, a magistrate, "Have you ever got anonymous letters accusing women?" replied, "We get lots of them."

it for some time said, touching with his finger a spot near the middle, " Sir, I think it will be *about there.*" Although he may have come within a minimum of the centre by this tentative method, his answer would by no means satisfy the geometrician, and in the same way it cannot satisfy the lover of justice that justice should probably be *about there*—for " Laws," as Junius says extremely well, " are intended not to trust to what men will do, but to guard against what they may do."

Thus we see that the statement which is so often made and accepted, that this law applies only to prostitutes, is calculated to exercise a blinding and confusing influence over the public mind in this question. It seems to be commonly assumed *that some decisive tribunal which has gone before has already decided that weighty matter* which marks out those who are fit subjects for the operation of this law ; and at other times it is assumed with an astonishing boldness on the part of some, and credulity on the part of others, either that these persons have by some overt act of their own marked themselves out as immoral characters, or that society possesses some divining-rod by which this class of persons may be distinctly marked off from all others. So far is this from being the case, that every one who has any experience of the poorer classes, knows that there is no point where an exact line of distinction can be drawn, but that there is every degree of shade between the absolutely virtuous woman and the most degraded and evident harlot. It is well known that among the poor there are thousands who are unchaste, but whom it would be an act of supreme injustice and cruelty to bring under this Act. And therefore this infringement of the constitutional forms of justice is the more to be deplored, considering the difficulty and delicacy of the distinctions of the cases which are by this Act brought before such a wretchedly inadequate tribunal as a single justice of peace, enlightened, not by facts, but by the credulity of a single policeman. Justices of the peace may be very good men, but they are not fitted to be sole and irresponsible judges in such a solemn and difficult question as they are required to determine under these Acts, nor, if we remember aright, has the generally received opinion of the character of "justice's justice" been usually such as to warrant the unlimited trust which we are here called on to repose in them. Even admitting that in every instance they are the best men in the world, they have, if we remember aright what the generally received opinion is, been believed to be rather liable to err,[1] and in any event we

---

[1] On the occasion of the trial of a young girl under these Acts in a certain town of Kent, a full bench of magistrates was assembled. She was condemned to a month's imprisonment, and on leaving the court remarked, "I did find it rather hard that the gentleman on

must still remember that sentence, already quoted, of Junius, that laws are intended not to trust to what justices of the peace will do, but to guard against what they may do. It is perfectly true certainly that jury-men are fallible as well as justices of the peace; nay, that they may be even in individual instances corrupt and foolish, but that form of trial, with its publicity, and all its other accompaniments, which has been found in other cases to be the necessary "bulwark of northern liberty," is not likely to be capable of being so easily dispensed with in this.[1]

For the rich and great there may be little danger in dispensing with jury trial in this particular instance. As there are classes in society whose position and wealth place them above any chance of being errone-ously accused of theft, so there are classes whose position, wealth, and surroundings place the women belonging to them equally above any chance of being erroneously accused of being prostitutes. To this fact we may probably trace the apathy and indifference of so many of the upper classes to the passing of the Contagious Diseases Acts, and the urbanity with which they assure us that our fears are ungrounded, and that

the bench who gave the casting vote for my imprisonment had paid me five shillings the day before to go with him !"

[1] Creasy's *Constitution*, pp. 225 and 227.

the operation of these Acts can seldom err. Again
we must quote the words of Junius, " Laws are intended not to trust to what men will do, but to guard
against what they may do."   But, at the same time, can
we accept the assurance that the action of the officials
who carry out these Acts will never be in error?   We
certainly cannot.   Ladies who ride in their carriages
through the streets at night are in little danger of
being molested.   But what of working women ?   What
of the daughters, sisters, wives of working men, out,
it may be on an errand of mercy, at night?   And
what, most of all, of that girl whose father, mother,
friends are dead, or far away, who is struggling hard,
in a hard world, to live uprightly and justly by
the work of her own hands,—is she in no danger
from this law?   Lonely, and friendless, and poor, is
she in no danger of a false accusation from malice or
from error ? especially since one clause of the Act particularly marks out *homeless* girls as just subjects for
its operation.   And what has she, if accused, to rely on,
under God, except that of which this law has deprived
her, the appeal to be tried " by God and my country;
by which she is understood to claim to be tried by a
jury, and to have all the judicial means of defence to
which the law entitles her."[1]

[1] De Lolme, p. 171.

It is not only however in the Act itself alone that we see this indifference to the interests of the poor and unprotected, whose sole protection under heaven lies in that constitution which this law has violated, but also in the carrying out of this law by the Admiralty and War Office, whom in place of the constitution which it has set aside it has erected as the guardians of the weak. By these tender guardians of the weak, we find an actual crusade carried on under this law against the defenceless. In the directions given at various times to the police, they are enjoined to keep an especial eye on the proceedings of "milliners, shop-girls, domestic servants," and the like. It is said that the beginning of strife is like the letting out of water : it is a process which when once begun is not so easily ended, and those who have opened the torrent cannot say where it will cease. The same may justly be said of the admission of a false principle into legislation, and when the barriers of constitutional safeguards are swept away by Act of Parliament, nothing can stem the torrent of illegality and oppression which will follow. I shall speak more hereafter of this consequence, and only here observe how the overreaching of a bad law is the necessary consequence of its own vicious nature.

We have been reproached for making this question a class question. We accept the reproach, if reproach it

be; because we say that it is a question for the poor
rather than for the rich. It was not we who initiated
this distinction, but the majority of the upper classes
soon taught us that they considered it no question of
theirs. They told us plainly that the subject was too
unpleasant to be treated as one of public interest; but
while with this plea they endeavoured to silence us, we
found that they generally lent the weight of their influence, and not always apathetically or ignorantly, to the
promotion of this legislation. To them this legislation
involved no present and immediate diminution of freedom for themselves, and they seem to have been blindly
ignorant or selfishly forgetful that their children and
children's children would be, as well as the children of
the poor, inheritors of the fatal consequences of violated
liberties; and that the chains which they now weave
for others will in time entangle themselves. But when
we turned to the humbler classes, we found that they
knew that it *is* a question for them; and that they,
more intelligent in this than the upper classes, knew
that it was also a question for this whole country of
England, whose political liberty depends on the preservation of the rights of all. "The trial by jury ever has
been," says Blackstone,[1] "and I trust ever will be,
looked upon as the glory of the English law. . . . It is

[1] Blackstone, Book iii, p. 378.

the most transcendent privilege that any subject can enjoy, or wish for, that he cannot be affected in his property, his liberty, or his person, but by the unanimous consent of twelve of his neighbours and equals,—a constitution that I may venture to affirm has, under Providence, secured the just liberties of this nation for a long succession of ages. And a celebrated French writer, who concludes that because Rome, Sparta, and Carthage have lost their liberties, therefore those of England in time must perish, should have recollected that Rome, Sparta, and Carthage, at the time when their liberties were lost, were strangers to the trial by jury." It is jury trial which, says he,[1] "preserves in the hands of the people that share which they ought to have in the administration of public justice, and prevents the encroachments of the more powerful and wealthy citizens." "And particularly," says he further, "it is a circumstance well worthy of an Englishman's observation, that in Sweden, the trial by jury, that bulwark of northern liberty, which continued in its full vigour so lately as the middle of the last century, is now fallen into disuse; and that there, though the regal power is in no country so closely limited, yet the liberties of the Commons are extinguished, and the government is degenerated into a mere aristocracy."[2]

[1] Blackstone, Book iii. p. 379.   [2] See Appendix A, p. 179.

I cannot therefore but regard the present as a crisis as great as any crisis through which this nation has ever passed. This country was once called on to decide whether it would permit the King for his satisfaction to override this 39th clause of Magna Charta, and it decided most emphatically that he should not. It is now called on to decide whether it will permit Parliament itself, for the sake of the lusts of certain men, to override this same clause.

It remains for the people of England to decide this question, and a very solemn choice is given to you, my countrymen, at this moment: Are these men to have protection in their vices, or will you retain your liberties?

If any of my readers, then, came to the consideration of this matter with the idea that there might be something to be said for this law medically, and that though there might be something undefinedly wrong in it, yet it embodied at least a benevolent intention, let him then remember that he has at the next election to answer this question for himself and his country: Shall we have liberty in lust, or shall we have political freedom? We cannot retain both.

CHAPTER III.

I NOW come to consider the cases to which I have before alluded, in which jury trial is dispensed with. I shall show their nature, and how the question to be decided under the Acts of Parliament to which we object in no way belongs to that class of questions.

Having one day explained the nature of these Acts to a working man, he appeared incredulous of their existence, and exclaimed, " This is impossible ! for every one in England can claim jury trial." I believe these words to be expressive of a misapprehension under which a vast number of people labour. This man's impression was true regarding the great principles of English legislation. But a supporter of these Acts might have answered him by telling him that there are in England a number of cases which are decided by a single justice of the peace without the intervention of a jury. Although perhaps at first silenced by this objection, and deprived, therefore, apparently of an obvious argument for claiming jury trial for the women accused under the Acts, our friend,

after more mature consideration, could not fail to come
to the conclusion that, after all, there was surely some
injustice here. In this conclusion he would be correct.

In a free country like England, where people are
brought up under just institutions, and where the principles of constitutional freedom are so universally
diffused in men's talk, actions, and thoughts that they
form the underlying spirit of all political and social
intercourse, the instincts of a person whose information
is no more definite than that which he gets from the
whole tone of society are in the main trustworthy and
just. These instincts are more to be relied upon than
legal subtleties, and are themselves the surest argument
for the justice of our constitution. It is the in-
extinguishable instinct of freedom, strengthened and
nourished by the existence of free institutions, which
constitutes the guarantee of the continuance of a
nation's liberty; and for this reason it is that I would
give much weight to those widely diffused and instinctive ideas, which we find even more amongst the
unlettered than amongst those classes whose sense of
freedom has been blunted by the enjoyment of exclusive and unquestioned privileges.

Under such circumstances as these, when an unjust
law comes to be argued and discussed by the public
generally, we find that a strong and universally diffused

appreciation of its unjust character may, and indeed always does, exceed the power of definitely pointing out the exact part of the constitution which may be violated by such a law. It is one of the blessings of this free country of England, that a perception of freedom and of constitutional right is more widely diffused than it is possible for a knowledge of the statute-book to be, or of the particular laws which form the basis of that constitution. The many are thus, by the education which they receive from our free institutions, made the protectors of our liberties, which could never be protected or maintained if in the hands only of the few and learned.[1] In accordance with this principle, we find the general instinctive perception of the violation of liberty by the Contagious Diseases Acts giving vent to itself throughout the country in varied forms, and in none more so than in an expression, which has not been unfrequently used, that these Acts are in some way or other opposed to the Habeas Corpus Act.

These Acts as they stand do not directly violate the Habeas Corpus Act, yet this very objection to them, erroneous though it may be in the absolute letter, serves only the more to show how widely diffused is a

[1] Lieber in his work on Civil Liberty remarks that lawyers have rarely been the promoters of reform in the laws : he excepts "the immortal Sir Samuel Romilly" and a few others.

true appreciation of the spirit in which the Habeas Corpus Act is conceived. The spirit of the Habeas Corpus Act, equally with that of Magna Charta, of which it is an elucidation, is violated by these Acts.

It is said in Magna Charta, "no man shall be taken, or imprisoned, or be disseised of his freehold or liberties or free customs, or be outlawed or exiled, or anyotherwise destroyed; nor will we pass upon him, nor condemn him, but by the lawful judgment of his peers, or by the law of the land. We will sell to no man, we will not deny or defer to any man, either justice or right."[1]

Now let us just again view these sentences as strictly applying to the administration of justice, in order to show the truth of the instinctive feeling above alluded to of so many people, that the Habeas Corpus Act is in some way violated.

"These words contain," says Sir E. Creasy,[2] "two great principles, the one that persons accused of criminal offences shall have free jury," of which I have already spoken, "the other, that no man shall be imprisoned on mere general grounds of suspicion at the discretion or caprice of the executive power; but that imprisonment shall be only inflicted as the result of a

[1] It is thus worded in the Charter of Henry III.
[2] *English Constitution*, p. 204.

legal trial and sentence, or for the purpose of keeping in safe custody, when necessary, an accused person on a definite charge, until he can be tried on that charge. This latter principle is familiar to us by the term of an Englishman's right to a Habeas Corpus, if his personal liberty be interfered with."

The Habeas Corpus Act, therefore, as thus explained, is distinctly one of the great constitutional safeguards against arbitrary imprisonment or detention; and this is undoubtedly the correct as well as the generally diffused understanding of the principle of that Act. And the readiness with which people refer to the Contagious Diseases Acts as a violation of the principle of the Habeas Corpus Act, is a proof of the fact that these Acts involve proceedings of a character unconstitutionally arbitrary.

The fact is, that to imprison a person without any trial at all would be a *literal* violation of the Habeas Corpus Act, but that to imprison a person after an inadequate trial by an inadequate tribunal, as these Contagious Diseases Acts do, is a violation of the *principle* of the Habeas Corpus Act just as great. Lord Coke says, " it is the worst oppression that is done by colour of justice;" and we cannot regard that imprisonment as any less a violation of the Habeas Corpus Act, because it is inflicted after a mode of trial, the adoption of which Parliament had no right, in this instance, to legalize.

We therefore see that the legalizing of a tribunal so inadequate for the judgment of cases so grave as those which under these Acts are submitted to a justice of the peace, is in effect a suspension by Parliament of the Habeas Corpus Act, and not, as is usual, for a limited time, but for an indefinite time, and for a vast proportion of Her Majesty's subjects. "The suspension of the Habeas Corpus Act is an expedient which," says Blackstone,[1] "ought only to be tried in cases of extreme emergency, for a short and limited time; and in these the nation parts with its liberty for a while in order to preserve it for ever."

Now it may be asked, How can we so strongly condemn this particular Act to which we are opposed, while at the same time there actually exists a set of cases, viz., those included in the category of summary proceedings, in which jury trial is equally dispensed with? Why, if the country be generally content to admit these, should it not be content to admit the Contagious Diseases Acts? I will proceed to answer this question.

I find in Blackstone an account of these innovations upon our ancient constitutional principles, which are

[1] Blackstone, vol. i. p. 145.

D

known by the name of summary proceedings. These summary proceedings are of comparatively recent origin, and I cannot give the reader a better account of them, and of what they involve, than by quoting what Blackstone says on the subject :[1]—

"By a *summary* proceeding, I mean such as is directed by several Acts of Parliament (for the common law is a stranger to it, unless in the case of contempts) for the conviction of offenders, and the inflicting of certain penalties created by those Acts of Parliament. In these there is no intervention of a jury, but the party accused is acquitted or condemned by the suffrage of such person only as the statute has appointed for his judge,—an institution designed professedly for the greater ease of the subject, by doing him speedy justice, and by not harassing the freeholders with frequent and troublesome attendances to try every minute offence. But it has of late been so far extended as, if a check be not timely given, to threaten the disuse of our admirable and truly English trial by jury, unless only in capital cases ; for—

"I. Of this summary nature are all trials of offences and frauds contrary to the laws of the *excise* and other branches of the *revenue,* which are to be inquired into and determined by the commissioners of the respective

[1] Blackstone, Book iv. chap. 20.

departments, or by justices of the peace in the country; officers who are all of them appointed and removable at the discretion of the Crown. And although such convictions are absolutely necessary for the due collection of the public money, and are a species of mercy to the delinquents, who would be ruined by the expense and delay of frequent prosecutions by action or indictment, and though such has usually been the conduct of the commissioners as seldom (if ever) to afford just grounds to complain of oppression; yet, when we again consider the various and almost innumerable branches of this revenue which may be in their turns the subjects of fraud, or at least complaints of fraud, and of course the objects of this *summary* and arbitrary jurisdiction, we shall find that the power of these officers of the Crown over the property of the people is increased to a very formidable height.

" II. Another branch of summary proceedings is that before *justices of the peace*, in order to inflict divers petty pecuniary mulcts and corporal penalties denounced by Act of Parliament for many disorderly offences, such as common swearing, drunkenness, vagrancy, idleness, and a vast variety of others, for which I must refer the student to the justice-books formerly cited, and which used to be formerly punished by the verdict of a jury in the court-leet. This change

in the administration of justice hath however had some
mischievous effects, as—1st, The almost entire disuse
and contempt of the court-leet and sheriff's tourn, the
King's antient courts of common law, formerly much
revered and respected.   2nd, The burthensome increase
of the business of a justice of the peace, which dis-
courages so many gentlemen of rank and character from
acting in the commission, from an apprehension that
the duty of their office would take up too much of
that time which they are unwilling to spare from the
necessary concerns of their families, the improvement
of their understandings, and their engagements in other
services of the public; though, if *all* gentlemen of
fortune had it both in their power and inclinations to
act in this capacity, the business of a justice of the
peace would be more divided, and fall the less heavy
upon individuals, which would remove what in the
present scarcity of magistrates is really an objection so
formidable that the country is greatly obliged to any
gentleman of figure who will undertake to perform that
duty, which in consequence of his rank in life he owes
more peculiarly to his country.   However, this back-
wardness to act as magistrates arising greatly from this
increase of summary jurisdiction is productive of, 3rd,
a third mischief, which is, that this trust, when slighted
by gentlemen, falls of course into the hands of those

who are not so, but the mere tools of office. And then the extensive power of a justice of the peace, which even in the hands of men of honour is highly formidable, will be prostituted to mean and scandalous purposes, to the low ends of selfish ambition, avarice, or personal resentment. And from these ill consequences we may collect the prudent foresight of our antient lawgivers, who suffered neither the property nor the punishment of the subject to be determined by the opinion of any one or two men; and we may also observe the necessity of not deviating any farther from our antient constitution by ordaining new penalties to be inflicted upon summary convictions."

Sir Edward Creasy also says on the same subject :— "The great constitutional principle of trial by jury is still respected so far as regards all trials for offences of a graver character, and which subject the person convicted of them to a severe punishment. . . . . But for upwards of a century the practice of exposing persons charged with minor offences to trial and summary conviction by one or two justices of the peace has been growing more and more prevalent. It is deeply to be regretted that so little heed has been paid to the sage and humane warnings of Blackstone against the increase of this system of withdrawing criminal charges from the consideration of a jury."

Mr. Justice Warren also speaks, in his abridgment and adaptation of Blackstone's *Commentaries*, respecting the "inroads on the noble institution of trial by jury which are now being made incessantly;" and he gives the following warning : "It is a matter of supreme concern to the country to beware of shaking the confidence of the humble classes of society in the administration of criminal justice, by infringing their right to an open and formal trial by their equals, and placing them at the mercy of, it may be, an interested and prejudiced superior." [1]

[1] Professor Sheldom Amos writes on this subject :—"The proceedings contemplated by the Contagious Diseases Acts have been placed among a large and rapidly growing class of proceedings only technically criminal, and instituted for quasi-moral, sanitary, fiscal, or general police purposes. To this class belong cab-regulations, regulations in respect of the cattle-plague, regulations for preventing nuisances in the way of obstructions in the street or on the pavement, regulations in the way of railway bye-laws for securing the safety of passengers, etc. The actions endeavoured to be prevented by the class of laws here involved are not crimes in the sense of being in themselves morally reprehensible, still less abominable, but they are crimes so far as they are absolutely forbidden by the State, and the punishment and prevention of them is undertaken by the State through its own officers. This class of Acts has been very much multiplied of late years, and the proceedings with respect to them are always in the first instance before one or two magistrates. Some of the proceedings are 'summary;' that is, the magistrate can assign the punishment at once without appeal ; others are summary only in the sense that the magistrate can, if the accused consent, assign the punishment at once, but the case can be reserved for Quarter Sessions and for jury trial in the event of the accused being able to find securities for his appearance.

While merely noticing in passing the grave objections of these eminent lawyers to the whole principle and operation of these summary convictions, I must draw the particular attention of my readers to the only excuse which these lawyers allow for this encroachment on constitutional rights, namely, the beneficent intention of expediting justice in minor cases for the sake of the individuals concerned.

From the quotations which I have given above, there are three main facts which may be gathered, viz., *first*, that summary proceedings *are* an encroachment on

Thus, you see that the claim to jury trial is already practically obsolete for all offences not of such kind as theft, robbery from the person, murder, assaults, treason, forgery, and such like atrocious forms of wrong-doing. The proceedings under the Contagious Diseases Acts are placed among the first of the classes above described, that is, summary proceedings without appeal. I think with you that the extension and multiplication of such Acts and proceedings is a grave constitutional peril, as I have said elsewhere." Let the reader compare the grave cases tried under the Contagious Diseases Acts with the quasi-moral, sanitary, and fiscal cases adverted to above, and let him mark the conclusions to which the framers of these Acts are inevitably driven through having placed these cases on this category. On the one hand, if, as some of our opponents say, these Acts are directed against vice, and are for the discouragement of the sin of prostitution, then, as we have seen, their framers are guilty of a violation of the constitution by placing cases of real criminality, involving severe penalties, on the list of summary proceedings in which there is no appeal. But if, as by far the greater number of our opponents affirm, these Acts do not treat prostitution as criminal, and these cases properly belong to the category above cited, then to what an awful moral conclusion are they driven on the other hand! To exact an exorbitant

liberty, and lamented over by great lawyers ; *second*, that
they are only for the sake of minor offences, and only
in that case tolerable ; and *third*, that there are cases
which, when included in this category, render these
encroachments especially dangerous, and by no manner
of means, or by any argument, to be tolerated.

Let the reader observe carefully these facts, and let
him also observe the reason why these summary convictions are allowed in minor cases—that is, for the
sake of the accused, and to expedite justice,—and let

fare or to drive recklessly in the streets is a legal offence in a cabman ;
but to take a fare within prescribed limits and to drive in the streets
is no moral offence at all. The same kind of argument holds true
of all the technical offences created by the Acts of Parliament above
alluded to. It is the exceeding of a certain limit (thereby causing inconvenience to society) which constitutes the legal offence under these
economic regulations. But in the Contagious Diseases Acts the case
is wholly different. Prostitution itself is morally criminal. The
State—placing the Contagious Diseases Acts on the category of
merely economical regulations—makes the crime dealt with under
them to consist in acting as a prostitute *when out of health.* It says
to the trader in sin, " You are guilty, unless you pursue this trade
under certain conditions prescribed by Act of Parliament," thus
plainly implying, " You are not guilty so long as you ply your trade
in compliance with the conditions imposed by our Act,"—hence the
fearfully immoral influence of such a law upon the people at large !
Whatever may be said, on the ground of expediency, against certain
recent Acts of Parliament, it can never be said that their influence
is *directly* immoral, for the technical definition by the State of the
crime treated in these cases does not involve the recognition of the
lawful and innocent character of actions in themselves vicious,
condemned by God's Word, and ruinous to society ; finally, it is
clear that little or no injury to character is incurred by a false
accusation under these economical Acts, whereas a false accusation
under the Contagious Diseases Acts is ruinous.

him ask himself whether he finds this motive inspiring these Acts. The answer to his inquiry will be, that the summary proceedings under these Acts are *not* for the sake of the accused, and that they are *not* to expedite justice.

If then for these intentions the danger is tolerated of the infringement of the strict letter of Magna Charta in these minor cases, can its principle therefore be permitted to be destroyed in a case where no such intentions are manifest ?

In the first place, the summary character of these Acts in question does not exist for the sake of the accused, as may be best shown by a provision under them called the " voluntary submission," by means of which a woman is made to criminate herself; whereas, in all other cases, care is taken in any examination of an accused person to give him every advantage, and not to entangle him; and he is especially advised by the person who examines him, to say or sign nothing to criminate himself. The woman, on the contrary, is subjected to no examination, but is simply requested to criminate herself; and the War Office and Admiralty order that if she do not immediately criminate herself, she is to be threatened with penal consequences for her refusal.[1]

[1] The practical working of this Act turns upon the voluntary submission. The clauses which refer to this are as follows :—
Act 1866, clause 17.—" Any woman, in any place to which this Act

In the second case, the proceedings under these Acts
are not for the sake of expediting the matter, and of
reinstating the accused in society, because this Act

applies, may voluntarily, by a submission in writing, signed by her in
the presence of, and attested by, the superintendent of police, subject herself to a periodical medical examination under this Act for
any period not exceeding one year."

Act 1869, clause 6.—"Where any woman in pursuance of the
principal Act (1866) voluntarily subjects herself by submission in
writing to a periodical medical examination under that Act, such
submission shall, for all the purposes of the Contagious Diseases
Acts 1866 to 1869, have the same effect as an order of a justice
subjecting the woman to examination, and all the provisions of the
principal Act respecting the attendance of the woman for examination, and her absenting herself to avoid examination, and her
refusing or wilfully neglecting to submit herself for examination,
and the force of the order subjecting her to examination after
imprisonment for such absence, refusal, or neglect shall apply and
be construed accordingly." If a woman do not desire to sign
the voluntary submission, the process under the Acts is that in
conformity with the clause 4, Act 1869, already cited, she shall
be summoned before a justice, by whom the question as to her
being a prostitute or not is first to be tried, and then if he is satisfied that she is such, she is ordered for examination. It is not
until after this process of law, and until she has absented herself
wilfully from the examination thus ordered, that there are any
penal consequences. (See clause 28, Act 1866, quoted below.)
The arbitrary character of the offices to which the carrying out
of these Acts is intrusted is to be seen from the orders given
by the War Office to the policeman, with respect to the voluntary submission, one of which orders is as follows :—" *Should any
woman object to sign, she is to be informed of the penal consequences
attending such refusal,* and the advantages of a voluntary submission are to be pointed out to her." *Now, there are no penal consequences legally attending such a refusal ;* on the contrary, *penal
consequences attend signing :* and the War Office here utterly ignores
all the process of law which intervenes between the accusation of

condemns her to be, or sign herself, a bondwoman for a given period not exceeding a year.[1]

Therefore the motives for making the proceedings under this Act summary cannot be said to exist.

With respect to the voluntary submission, the illegal threat of the Admiralty and War Office (already quoted in the Note, p. 58), backed up by police intimidation, has induced many women, friendless and ignorant of the laws, to sign that submission in preference to the alternative of going before a magistrate. To this they have been induced by the hope that their

the woman, under clause 16, Act 1869, and the penal consequences which, according to clause 28, Act 1866, may under certain circumstances ensue. Perhaps nothing could be such a striking comment as this on the utterly flimsy character of the whole process of law to which the woman is subjected. The War Office has here leapt at once from the suspicion of a policeman to the woman's condemnation, as if the suspicion of a policeman alone were sufficient proof of her being a prostitute. Indeed, under the Act it seems fundamentally to be assumed that policemen are infallible judges as to whether a woman is chaste or not.

[1] The form of the voluntary submission is as follows :—" I —— voluntarily subject myself to a periodical medical examination by the visiting surgeon for —— calendar months." In order to put it more plainly before the reader, let him imagine some petty misdemeanour, such as petty theft or disorderly conduct,—let him imagine a paper of a self-criminating character put before the accused, wherein he signs words to this effect: " I —— submit myself to (here mentioning some new form of punishment, which shall include the public registration of his calling as a thief or a drunkard) for —— calendar months." Where is here the desirable expediting of justice ? and where is here the " benevolent motive of setting the culprit, after a brief punishment, free to start a new life " ?

registration may thus be kept a secret, and by ignorance of the real nature of the personal outrage to which they submit themselves, the real nature of which it is impossible for any one to gather from the form of the voluntary submission, or, indeed, from anything in the Acts.[1] But if it be alleged, as an inference from this, that the ordeal incurred is not so detestable a thing to a woman as we have represented it to be, if they choose rather to submit to it voluntarily than to have their case tried openly before a magistrate, choosing a certainty of subjection to this ordeal rather than publicity, with the chance of escape ; and if on that account it be alleged in objection to our argument, that the publicity of open jury trial would be still more painful for these women to encounter than the publicity of proceedings before a single magistrate, we would reply that, though the alternative just mentioned is offered by the Act, it is by no means the alternative which has been presented to the minds of the women, to whom the lie circulated by the authority of the Admiralty and War Office has distinctly declared that the going before a magistrate is only a public method of the same submission ; and to whose mind that going before the

---

[1] When the gross nature of the outrage involved in the examination becomes known to them, many refuse to sign the voluntary submission a second time, and have to be taken before a magistrate.

magistrate is presented, not as a trial, but as a proceeding involving direct penal consequences. If it be represented to her that it is penal to refuse to sign the voluntary submission, how can she refuse? Yet even though no such representation were made, and though every woman had direct access to the Act of Parliament thus falsely interpreted to her, it must still be apparent to every honest mind that it is a gross parody of justice to offer to any person an insufficient or partial tribunal on the one hand, and, on the other, the opportunity of self-crimination. It is a base and unjust alternative, and one which ought not to be presented to any citizen of a free country, and, above all, ought not to be presented in this particular case ; for, be it observed, such an alternative and such a method of trial gives rise to a recklessness of accusation peculiarly grievous in the present instance, and which the system in question seems framed precisely to foster,—a recklessness of accusation which would be checked by the fear which must affect even the most powerful individual in the State, and make him reflect well before he too lightly brings any accusation against any one, knowing that the truth of that accusation must be examined and decided by twelve indifferent men, not appointed till the hour of trial, and not by those paid officials accustomed to believe in the truth of such accusations, and

knowing that when once the fact of a false accusation
is ascertained the law must of course redress it.

Let me, however, at this point remind the reader, that
my argument throughout is not a plea to retain these
Acts, amended by the introduction of the safeguard of
jury trial; but that my object is to bring them to the
test of this ancient and sacred institution, and to show
that since they cannot exist in conjunction with it, then
these Acts stand condemned thereby, and therefore
must be expunged from the statute-book.

The question now arises, Is this at all a fit case for
summary proceeding, even although those proceedings
did in this case expedite the celerity of justice? Now,
if we refer back to the quotations already made on this
subject from Blackstone and others, we shall see that
the abridgment of legal safeguards is only to be permitted in what are called minor cases. And the cases
to be treated under these Acts can by no means be
called minor cases, for reasons which I am about to
give. First, however, let it be carefully observed that
there are two distinct proceedings under the Act, the
first being that of which I have treated in the preceding chapter, namely, the determination as to whether
the woman be a prostitute or not; and the second,
with which I am not dealing here, being that which
is directed against the offence created under the Acts,

that offence being the carrying on of the trade of a prostitute otherwise than under the conditions imposed by Government. And what we are here particularly objecting to is the making the first proceeding, above referred to, a summary proceeding, and calling that case a minor case which relates to the determination as to whether a woman is immoral or not.

I have thought it right to make this distinction clear because of our adversaries, who, when we speak of the punishment under these Acts inflicted on women, affect to suppose that we refer only to the punishment inflicted on a prostitute for the offence of not obeying the Government conditions; again here assuming, as they invariably do, that no one but such a person is ever dealt with by this law; so that I must again emphatically call the attention of the reader to the fact, that the first proceeding under the Act is that of determining, by the arbitrary tribunal which I have before discussed, the fact as to whether the woman be a prostitute or not. And if the decision of this tribunal be, as we declare it is and must be, very frequently erroneous, it is a virtuous woman, and not a prostitute, who is involved in all the subsequent proceedings; and since these proceedings are entered upon on account of her resistance to the subsequent action of the law, the chance of gross injustice is all the greater, since it certainly would be the virtuous woman, or one who had some modesty left, rather than the vicious one, who would resist the proceedings.

How then can that be called a minor offence, which involves by no means a minor penalty? How can that be called a case for the law's celerity, which involves a repeated, and it may be a life-long, imprisonment?[1] How can that be called a minor case which involves not only repeated imprisonment, but which is based on an accusation of the most subtle, cruel, and injurious kind, and which, even though disproved, carries with it its own penalty, whether in the form of loss of charracter (which character is often the sole capital of a poor woman), or violation of the person of that outrageous kind which I have before said it is impossible to mention?—a violation which is in fact such a proceeding as is forbidden in the clause of Magna Charta as above quoted, " and neither will we destroy any one except by the judgment of his peers." How can that be regarded as a minor offence which involves a punishment which is irretrievable, and which is the only irretrievable punishment now inflicted in this country except that of death? It is in vain for supporters of the Acts to deny that the violation of the person above alluded to is punishment of the grossest and most

[1] See Chapter v.

horrible kind for every creature calling herself a woman :
but should anybody urge that that operation of the Act
upon the person of a proved prostitute is neither
horrible nor irretrievable, once more let him remember
that these Acts deal with women generally, not with
prostitutes exclusively, and that the first process under
the Acts is the arbitrary determination as to the character of the woman suspected, which determination
amounts in fact to an arbitrary selection of such women
as the policeman and magistrate deem proper to bring
under the Acts.

In the case of minor offences, it is the proportionately
trifling nature of the punishment inflicted which justi-
fies, if anything can justify, the summary conviction;
but such conviction cannot possibly in a free country
be tolerated, when the punishment consequent on conviction is of a nature so injurious and irretrievable.
If you deprive a man of life the punishment is irretrievable; no recompense can be made for it if erroneously
inflicted; hence in some countries punishment by death
is on this very account prohibited when the evidence is
only circumstantial. What then shall we say of a
case in which an irretrievable punishment is inflicted
where there is no necessary circumstantial evidence
at all, but suspicion only, and further, without the safeguard, which the law applies in the other case, of jury

trial? What can atone to an innocent woman for the destruction of her character brought about by mere suspicion, and without the chance of the time-honoured appeal "to God and my country"? What can atone to her for the personal outrage, which is made so light of by some doctors, but which, whether inflicted by any private villain, or by a gentleman paid by the Government to inflict it, must bring to every decent woman unmitigated shame and anguish?

We therefore claim that these cases under this Act shall not be summarily treated as minor cases, because, to put it in the light least favourable to ourselves, no one can prove to us that an innocent woman may not be accused under it; and, being so accused, if punished wrongfully, she suffers more than any other person punished wrongfully would suffer; she has therefore more than any other person the right to all the safeguards which the law can offer. Now, it is admitted by all great lawyers that the supreme safeguard against accused persons being wrongfully punished, or against persons being wrongfully accused, is the existence of jury trial. These women, therefore, more than any other accused people, are entitled to have every legal safeguard. It is more tyrannical than can for a moment be endured in England, that such cases should be classed among minor cases, and be treated in the same summary fashion as when a little boy breaks windows.[1]

Now, let us ask our opponents " why, in this matter, did they dispense with jury trial ?" The only answer they could consistently give is, that if jury trial were adopted, the law would not work. If that be so, these Acts are condemned by that very admission. This test distinguishes at once the case in question from all other summary cases, for let us suppose any other case whatsoever now comprised among these treated as summary cases to be brought to the test of jury trial, and let us see what would be the result. It would be, not the miscarriage of the case, but the clearer and fuller establishment of justice, though at the expense of delay and the employment of greater machinery than the case might perhaps demand. The real reason for dispensing with this safeguard, however, we suspect is to be found in the same selfishness which prompted the Act, namely, that tender regard for the erring man, which

[1] Not only is the case treated summarily under the Contagious Diseases Acts, and thus the safeguard of jury trial taken away, but even the safeguards which are generally allowed in summary cases are taken away. In other summary cases, where the imprisonment adjudged shall exceed one month, there is the right of appeal to the the general or quarter sessions (see Appendix). But even this appeal is not allowed under the Contagious Diseases Acts, although (see clause 7, Act 1869, and clause 26, Act 1866) the woman may be imprisoned for nine months, and (see clause 28, Act 1866) may be imprisoned for three months with hard labour.

is by no means extended to either the frail or the virtuous woman. It would manifestly be inconvenient and disagreeable to those gentlemen, for whose fancied benefit these Acts were made, to be constantly in danger of being called up as witnesses to the immoral character of certain of their female companions, it may be of some poor girl introduced by their seduction into the paths of vice. For it is, unfortunately for them, a maxim of the Common Law of England, "that the best evidence the nature of the case will admit of shall always be required, if possible to be had,"[1] and the best and most direct evidence in this case is very clearly that of the male accomplices of the woman whose character is the subject of trial; wherefore we do not need to go far to discover why it is that the persons who have found it needful to make these Acts should have also found it needful to do away with jury trial.

For these reasons, and for others to be cited in an ensuing chapter, I can characterize these Acts as nothing other than a gross violation of the constitution of this country, whereby there is established a sort of press-gang, by which women are pressed into the ranks of vice by the shortest and easiest way possible, for the purpose of serving the lusts of men.

[1] Blackstone, Book iii. p. 367.

CHAPTER IV.

I SHALL in this chapter give some portion of a debate which took place in the House of Lords in the year 1736, on the occasion of an attempt made by Parliament to introduce a Bill against smugglers, so curiously similar in many points to the Acts under discussion, that I feel it not needful to apologize for introducing it in the present Essay, but call the reader's attention very markedly to the whole matter, inasmuch as many arguments which have been advanced, on one side or the other, in the discussion in which we are now engaged, were also advanced there, as the reader can himself see.

The case in point was a Bill to prevent smuggling, which enacted that upon information being given upon oath before any one justice of the peace, that any persons, to the number of three or more, were assembled to assist in smuggling, the justice might commit them without bail.

The great similarity, even of the very wording of this

to the Acts which we oppose, will be evident to the
reader; but I must point out that this bill against
smugglers was infinitely less grievous than these Acts,
inasmuch as the action of the justice of the peace here
extended only to unbailable imprisonment before trial,
which was followed in time by the regular course of
jury trial.

Lord Hardwicke, whose speech I quote, was a Crown
lawyer in the reign of George II., and while calling attention to every part of his speech, I would particularly mark the concluding paragraph, where every word,
with the mere alteration of a name, is directly applicable
to the question we are now discussing.

*Cobbett's Parliamentary History; debate in the Lords
on the Bill to Prevent Smuggling, May* 15, 1736.—" The
said bill was read for the first and second time in the
House of Lords, without any considerable debate, but
when it came before the committee several amendments were offered by Lord Hardwicke."

Lord Hardwicke spoke as follows:—" I am very
sensible how much it concerns us to prevent that
fraudulent and pernicious practice called smuggling,
and therefore I shall always be ready to join in such
measures as I think proper and necessary for that purpose; but at the same time, my Lords, do not let us
forget the freedom of our constitution, and the liberties

and privileges of the people; for slavery would be a
price too dear even for the most absolute security
against smuggling.[1] For this reason, when any
method is proposed, or bill brought in for the
detecting, apprehending, and punishing persons guilty
of such practices, we ought to consider, not only
whether it will be effectual for the benefit proposed, but
whether it will be consistent with our constitution and
the liberties of the people. By all those who understand anything of our constitution, it must be granted
that one of the greatest barriers for the liberties of the
people is that fundamental maxim of the laws of this
kingdom by which every man is presumed innocent
till the contrary appears by some overt act of his own,
and that act must be such an one as is itself unlawful,
and of such a nature that no innocent construction can
be put upon it. We have in our laws no such thing as
a crime by implication, nor do we pretend to judge of
or to punish a man for mere thinking. From hence it
is that a wicked or malicious intention can never with
us be proved by witnesses.[2] Facts only are admitted

---

[1] If the reader will in the following speech substitute the words
"Contagious Disease" for "Smuggling," and make several consequent alterations, he will find that this address stands as that of a
man rising from the dead to plead on our behalf.

[2] Compare with this, clause 4, Act 1869, where information is to
be lodged against a woman of whom the policeman has "good cause
to believe" that she has been "outside of those limits *for the purpose*

to be proved, and the judge and jury are from these facts to determine with what intention they were committed. But no judge or jury can ever by our laws suppose, much less determine, that an action in itself innocent or indifferent was attended with a criminal intention. Such an inference, my Lords, was never made in a free country, nor under any government but that of a tyrannical as well as arbitrary administration.

" Another security for our liberties is that no subject can be imprisoned unless some felonious and high crime be sworn against him. If the crime be not in itself atrocious, or if there be only a suspicion sworn against him, the greatest hardship he can be subjected to is to be imprisoned till he gives bail for his appearance ; and if any of our inferior judges refuse to admit him to bail, the subject so aggrieved may immediately apply by Habeas Corpus to the King's Courts in Westminster Hall, the judges of which are now, by the late happy Revolution, put above being influenced by any authority but that of justice and the established laws of the country ; nor awed by anything but that of their own reputation or an impeachment in Parliament, which would certainly be the consequence if they refused

of prostitution." The reader will observe that the policeman here has not suspicion necessarily of any act perpetrated, but merely he has suspicion that this woman harbours in her breast a certain intention.

justice to any of the least of his Majesty's subjects.
This, my Lords, with respect to private persons; is the
very foundation-stone of all our liberties, and if we
remove it, if we but knock off a corner, we may very
probably overturn the whole fabrick.

"Having premised these observations upon our constitution, and upon the nature of a free government, give
me leave, my Lords, to apply them to that clause in this
bill which subjects every man[1] in this kingdom to the
danger, nay, I may say certainty, of being committed to
prison by a single justice of peace, without bail or main-
prize, and of being convicted and transported as a
smuggler; and all this without his having been guilty
of any one overt act, except that of travelling properly
armed for his defence, and having perhaps the misfor-
tune to meet with two of his friends upon the road
armed in the same manner, in case any two[2] rogues of
informers shall swear that this honest man and his
friends were assembled and armed in order to be aiding
and assisting in the landing of prohibited goods.   This
regulation, when stripped of that multiplicity of words

[1] If Lord Hardwicke could use this language in respect to the
danger which every honest man was subjected by a law directed
against smugglers only, how much more are we justified in saying
that every woman encounters dangers of as grave a kind by the
existence of a law directed against unchaste women?

[2] Only *one* witness is required under the Contagious Diseases
Acts.

which render obscure the meaning and interest of every
clause of an Act of Parliament, really seems to me to
be the most terrible and the most entrapping regulation
that was ever proposed in any country. If it passes
into a law, I am sure it will not be quite safe for any
three gentlemen in the kingdom to be seen in company
together.   It is evident at first view that this regulation is repugnant to all the maxims of free government.
The wearing of arms is in itself an act not only innocent but commendable, therefore no presumption of any
crime can thence be inferred.[1]   And for this reason
the admitting of witnesses to prove that any three men
were so armed for purposes of smuggling, is admitting
witnesses to prove an intention without any one overt
act from whence that intention can possibly be inferred,
which is inconsistent with the freedom of our constitution and with the whole tenor of the laws of this kingdom.   We may as well admit witnesses to prove that a
man got up in the morning and put on his clothes in
order to assist in the running of goods, which I am sure
would be ridiculous as well as pernicious ; but this is

[1] How easily an innocent action may be misconstrued under the
Contagious Diseases Acts may be seen by the evidence of Mr. Par-
sons, an examining surgeon under these Acts, who when examined
by the Parliamentary Committee as to his definition of a prostitute
(there being none under the Acts), defined it as "any woman whom
there is fair and reasonable grounds to suspect to be *going* to places
which are the resort of prostitutes, and at times when immoral
persons are out," and added, "It is a matter of *mannerism* more
than anything else."

not all the hardship of the case : witnesses are not only to be admitted to prove a wicked intention without an overt act, but they are rewarded for giving such testimony,[1] which is a most dangerous practice, and a practice we have lately got too much into ; for, in my opinion, no man ought to be admitted as a witness against any criminal if he be to have any share of the payment on his conviction ;[2] however, in no case is it so dangerous as it will be in this, because when false witnesses come to swear a *fact* upon a man which he is innocent of, he may prove himself to have been at another place at the time, or he may fall upon many other ways to make his innocence appear, and to convict the witnesses of perjury, and this is in all other cases a great guard to the innocent ; but in the present case I should be glad to know how it will be possible for a man to prove that he had no such *intention* as is sworn against him, or to convict a false witness of perjury.[3]

[1] The only witness required under the Contagious Diseases Acts is the paid spy.

[2] A woman may be detained for nine months at a time in hospital, on evidence given by the hospital surgeon only (see clause 22, Act 1866, and clause 7, Act 1869) ; and the hospital authorities, whose servant he is, receive £30 a year for every bed which is filled.

[3] If the difficulty of proving innocence in this case be so great, we may consider the difficulty much greater for a woman to prove, not only that she had no intention of an evil nature, but that she is in fact a chaste woman. It has been said that it is impossible even for Diana herself to prove her own chastity.

"With respect, my Lords, to the security of the subject against unjust imprisonment, and with respect to the liberty of applying to the King's Courts, these valuable privileges are all to be taken away by this new regulation; a man is to be imprisoned without so much as a pretence of his having been guilty of any crime,[1] only because a sorry fellow perhaps has gone and sworn before a country justice, out of malice, that he intended to assist in the running of goods; and though by our constitution every man has a right to insist that in such cases no extravagant bail shall be exacted from him, yet now he is to be committed without bail, there to remain till he can force the justice, and his informer, to bring him to a trial, which I do not see how he can do, for by this clause the Habeas Corpus Act seems to be repealed. Again, if the justice should commit iniquity, either in not admitting of a proper and full vindication, or in delaying to bring the person accused to trial, where shall such person apply for relief? For the power of relief is by this clause taken from the King's Courts, and is given to the justices of the peace, who are removeable at the pleasure of a minister, and may, most of them, be made the drudging tools of an administration. *Therefore I must think it very extra-*

---

[1] In a recent pamphlet, one of the supporters of the Contagious Diseases Acts says of the women, "No *crime* is laid to their charge!" See Lane's answer to Duncan M'Laren.

ordinary, and inconsistent with the principles of the Revolution, to give such powers to such judges, or to give them any supreme and uncontrollable power whatsoever, especially in cases where the liberty of a subject is in immediate danger.

" *I am very certain that if ever I should see such a law passed I should look upon our constitution as at an end.* Yet we may have an administration that would be fond of having such a law passed, perhaps in order to guard against those treasonable practices which their own conduct had made frequent, and in such a case would not this very law be a good precedent for them, would not they have reason to say to Parliament, ' What! will you refuse to grant that security against treasonable practices which your ancestors have granted against the practice of smuggling?'"

After having proposed important amendments, Lord Hardwicke proceeded to say :—

" These amendments will, in my opinion, in some measure prevent those dangers which may accrue with respect to the freedom of our constitution and the liberty of the subject. I say, my Lords, in some measure, for neither these amendments, nor any amendments, can prevent its being a very dangerous bill, and such an one as I am sorry to see necessary in this once happy kingdom. It is one absolutely repugnant to the whole tenor of our laws, and inconsistent with the liberty and happiness of the people."

"I know, my Lords, it may be said that no man can be absolutely safe from treachery and perjury; but from all our law-books I defy any man to suppose a case where it is so easy to cook up a treacherous yet feasible accusation against one who has not been guilty of the least imprudence,[1] or so safe to give a false testimony as it will be in the case I have now laid before you. For in all or most other cases there must be a confederacy or combination between two or more persons in order to get a man convicted upon a false information, in which case the confederates are in danger of being betrayed by one another; and even the facts themselves, which are falsely sworn against a man, often furnish him with the means for justifying himself, and condemning his accusers, whereas in the present case there is no need of any confederacy, nor can the person accused justify himself by any means I can think of.[2]

"Upon the whole, my Lords, I must think this bill one of the most severe and dangerous bills that was

---

[1] This is precisely what we say of the Acts which we oppose.

[2] The malicious whisper of a single man, under the Contagious Diseases Acts, may destroy the character of a woman. A gentleman who lately visited Paris was sitting in the boulevards with a young Frenchman, who, observing a great many young women passing, remarked to his English companion, "I could have any one of these sent to prison to-morrow by a single word to the inspector of police."

ever passed by a British legislature, and yet notwithstanding its severity I am afraid it will be very far
from answering the end in view. I am afraid that
instead of preventing smuggling it will render hardy
and desperate all those who shall hereafter embark in
that pernicious trade, which will make them more bold
and enterprising than they ever were heretofore, and
their common danger will unite them closer together,
which will make them more powerful and formidable.
. . . By such laws we may ruin our constitution, we may
subject ourselves to arbitrary power, but even arbitrary
power itself will not prevent smuggling; for in France,
where arbitrary power has long been established, where
the punishment of every sort of smuggling is death or
the galleys, where they keep up a particular sort of
army called *les maltôtiers* for that very purpose, yet
smuggling is in that kingdom as frequent as in England, and their smugglers are much more desperate than
ours, for they march in little armies, are well armed
and disciplined, and often engage in battle with the
custom-house officers and the maltôtiers. The gentlemen of the French army are indeed but seldom employed in such exploits; they think it beneath them to
engage against banditti or to hunt after criminals; this
low sort of work they look on as fit only for maltôtiers
or sheriffs'-officers, and though they have a vast number

of such in France, yet with them and with all the other
advantages they have, it has never yet been in their
power to prevent smuggling."[1]

To this speech of Lord Hardwicke a reply was
made abounding in arguments, which bear a remarkable similarity to those used now against us by our
opponents, of which I will merely give the following
specimens :—" I shall readily agree, my Lord," says the

[1] Let the reader compare this with the description of the state of
Paris given by M. Le Cour himself, the Prefect of the Police Médi-
cale. There is a staff of special police appointed for the "surveil-
lance" of the public women. It is a post which is despised by the
more respectable men who take the office of regular police. These
women-hunters or "Mouchards" are intrusted with large and
arbitrary powers for hunting down and imprisoning these women.
What is the effect ? Is prostitution thereby restrained ? I quote
Le Cour's own words (*Prostitution in London and Paris*, 1789-1870,
by M. Le Cour) :—"These public women are everywhere, in the
drinking shops, the music saloons, the theatres, the balls ; they
haunt the public establishments, the railway stations and carriages,
they push respectable women off the pavement, they roll in carriages,
they frequent the Bois de Boulogne, they plant themselves outside
every coffee-house, they drive slowly along the footpaths, there is a
place by the lady's side which she seems to offer to the passer-by ;
there are hotels which freely open their doors to them at any hour
if they do not come alone." As with the French smugglers spoken
of by Lord Hardwicke, the rigour under which they lived gave rise
to an *esprit de corps* which enabled them to brave the authorities,
so do the most vicious persons in Paris band themselves together
as a compact community to defy authority. To quote Le Cour
again : " Panderers are numerous at Paris, where they find more
than anywhere else in the world the opportunity of practising their
manœuvres and escaping the attention of the authorities. They keep
registrary offices and restaurants, they sell articles for the toilet,
millinery, gloves, or perfumes, and they constitute true snares for

supporter of the Smuggling Act, in reply to Lord Hardwicke, "that we ought to be extremely cautious in
granting any new powers which may any way encroach
on the constitution or upon the liberties of the people;
but if we make a phantom of every new power and
new penalty that may be necessary, and give a loose to
our imaginations by supposing that every such power
or penalty will be made a wrong and unjust use of,
and turned towards the oppression and ruin of the
subject, instead of being applied to their relief and
preservation, we shall never grant any new power; for
no power was ever granted, nor can be granted, upon
which a fruitful imagination may not form various
scenes of horror and destruction;[1] nay, no power
can be granted but what may truly be made a wrong
use of, but while we have a Parliament subsisting,
while we are subjected to no earthly power but what
depends upon Parliament, we have no occasion to
frighten ourselves with such chimeras."

After he has shown to his own satisfaction, as our

all young girls who are engaged as workwomen and employées."
Mme. Daubie also says in her book, *La Femme Pauvre*, that panderers
and procurers band themselves together in such a compact *corps
d'élite* that they are able to engage the best houses in the city on
the best terms, and to oppose any measures adopted by the authorities which may seem to be unfavourable to their abominable traffic.

[1] Compare this with the *Saturday Review* and *Pall Mall Gazette*
remarks about "shrieking sisterhoods."

F

opponents also do, that under the Act complained of no
innocent person has anything to fear, and after he has
assured Lord Hardwicke that the justices are not in
the least likely to judge wrongly, for the excellent
reason that " if they did so they would be very derelict
in their duty," he goes on to use the very same argument which the supporters of the Acts which we oppose
have lately been very fond of using.   They affirm
that many a raw girl, trembling on the verge of evil
courses, being brought under the Acts, is terrified back
into a virtuous life by the penalties which she is made
to undergo.   Similarly Lord Hardwicke's opponent
argues : " A month's confinement in a correction-house,
with the severest sort of whipping, would be very far
from being an adequate punishment for the first
offence."   But such is his opinion of the reclamatory
effects of this beneficent process that he adds, " A raw
country fellow, or a poor labouring man, may for a
reward easily be drawn into assisting in the running
of goods, where no violence is intended, and may for
that purpose be prevailed on to loiter and wait somewhere near the sea coasts ; for such a man a month's
confinement and whipping may be a sufficient admoni-
tion ; he may be thereby reclaimed and frightened from
ever engaging again in such practices."

[1] *Parliamentary History*, vol. ix. p. 1253.

To these and similar arguments it was replied by
Lord Chancellor Talbot:—"My Lords, we are fully
sensible that it is the duty of Parliament to grant a
revenue sufficient for supporting the Government,[1] and
to contrive such methods of collecting the revenue as
may be effectual; but we likewise know that it is the
duty of Parliament to support the constitution, and to
preserve the liberties of the people; therefore, when it
begins to appear that the methods prescribed by Parliament are not effectual for the end intended, nor can be
made so without endangering our constitution, those
methods ought not to be further pursued. . . . It is
always with regret and sorrow, my Lords, that I form
to myself any apprehensions of danger to my native
country, and therefore I shall always avoid it as much
as possible; but we have already created so many new
crimes and transgressions, and have inflicted so many
new pains and penalties for preventing those transgressions, that, in my opinion, the fears of increasing them
can in no case be called phantoms. Our Parliaments
have, it is true, been hitherto able, generally speaking,
to give a check to every wrong use of any power and to
bring the offenders to punishment; and while our Parliament continues to be independent of those who have

---

[1] It had been urged that the customs could not be collected unless
the Bill against smugglers was passed.

the exercise of power,[1] their will, as well as their ability,
will continue the same. But we know the effect of
pains and penalties in other countries; we know that
Parliaments, Senates, and Assemblies have, by such
means, been made subservient to the worst and most
tyrannical uses that could be made of power;[2] and if
this should ever unfortunately happen to be our case,
our Parliaments will neither be willing nor able to
check the abuse of any power, or to punish the offenders. For this reason, we ought to be extremely jealous
of loading our people with pains and penalties, and
subjecting them to a multitude of penal laws; for
oppression may be easily cloaked under an Act of
Parliament, and many may be punished, under pretence
of their having been guilty of some action made penal
by Statute without raising any general murmur among
the people, or giving alarm to those who think *themselves*
in no danger from any such prosecution. Whereas the
least act of oppression without the pretence of Parlia-

---

[1] It would seem that Parliament is not now independent of the
permanent Officers of State, as, for instance, the authorities at the
Horse Guards.

[2] Compare this with what Blackstone says when speaking of the
operations of just law being necessarily slow ; that arises, says he,
from "liberty, property, civility, commerce, and an extent of popu-
lous territory, which whenever we are willing to exchange for
tyranny, poverty, barbarism, idleness, and a barren desert, we may
then enjoy the same despatch of causes as is so highly extolled in
some foreign countries."

ment would raise a general murmur and an universal alarm, because every man in the kingdom would then think himself in danger. In this nation no man of common sense would extend his power of oppression to any great length till he had got a Parliament to his mind; but when he has got such a Parliament, his power will then be without control, and by subjecting multitudes of our people to high pains and penalties, and the danger of being prosecuted upon penal Statute, we may render it easy for a man to accomplish this end, which, when once accomplished, may be by the same methods easily preserved as long as he pleases.

"No law can be proposed, my Lords, for the necessity of which some reasons may not be urged; even the most tyrannical laws have been made under the pretence of preventing some real abuse.[1]   But all wise nations have chosen to allow an abuse to escape unpunished rather than to make such a law as might possibly involve the innocent in the same punishment with the guilty.

"If ever any such custom or law should come to be established in this kingdom, the happiness and security of our people would be at an end; we might expect some-

---

[1] The pretence of the Contagious Diseases Acts may be reckoned as the lowest possible pretence, for it is that of attempting to preserve a man from the bodily inconveniences attending vicious habits, which by his own will he could avoid.

time or other to have informers as numerous and frequent in our streets, and in all public places, as ever the 'delatores' or informers were about Rome under their most tyrannical emperors.

" I shall grant that if the justice of peace understands the spirit of our laws, and acts justly, he will examine the informer narrowly as to circumstances, and will not commit unless the informer gives good reasons against those he informs against. But the words of this clause make no such precautions necessary. We are not now to inquire what the justice *ought* to do, but what he *may* do, and I *will* say that by these words, an information on oath will be a sufficient authority for the commitment, and will excuse the justice from all the penalties of false imprisonment.

" May we not suppose that such informations may be cooked up, and persons of great credit committed ? . . . Can we say that any subject is safe who *may* upon malicious information which he cannot disprove be brought into such danger? I say, my Lords, on information which he cannot disprove, for this will always be the case."

Such were the arguments used for and against the Bill about smuggling.

It is needless to point out to my readers how the same principles have ever in the history of similar struggles given rise to the same arguments, and the same actions.

It is impossible not to ask, with a feeling of sorrow and almost of fear for our country, " Where were the great lawyers in the House of Peers when this last most unconstitutional law was allowed to pass?　How was it that they, unlike their noble predecessors, sat silent while our liberties were thus being treacherously invaded?　Had they no word for justice if not for mercy?　and had they no power of discernment with regard to the future woes which such legislation entails?" There was an appeal once made in the House of Peers, whose echoes seem to have died away from the chamber of that assembly : I cannot conclude this chapter better than by quoting it.　Echoes which have ceased to be heard inside that House may be revived perhaps less fruitlessly outside its walls.

In a question which involved (like the Acts against which we contend) immoral as well as unconstitutional principles, it had been alleged that "it is justifiable to use every means that God and nature put into our hands."　To this Lord Chatham replied :[1]—

" I am astonished ! shocked ! to hear such principles confessed—to hear them avowed in this House, or in

[1] Speech delivered by Lord Chatham on the 20th November 1777.

this country, principles equally unconstitutional, in-human and unchristian ! My Lords, I did not intend to have encroached again upon your attention, but I cannot repress my indignation. I feel myself impelled by every duty. My Lords, we are called upon as mem-bers of this House, as Christian men, to protest against such notions standing near the throne, polluting the ear of majesty. 'Means that God and nature put into our hands !' I know not what ideas that lord may enter-tain of God and nature ; but I know that such abomin-able principles are equally abhorrent to religion and humanity. . . . These abominable principles, and this more abominable avowal of them, demand the most decisive indignation. I call upon that right reverend bench, those holy ministers of the Gospel, and pious pastors of our Church ; I conjure them to join in the holy work, and vindicate the religion of their God. I appeal to the wisdom and the law of this learned bench to defend and support the justice of their country. I call upon the bishops to interpose the unsullied sanctity of their lawn, upon the learned judges to interpose the purity of their ermine, to save us from this pollution ! I call upon the honour of your Lordships to reverence the dignity of your ancestors, and to maintain your own. I call upon the spirit and humanity of my country to vindicate the national character ! I invoke the genius of the constitution. . . . My Lords, this awful subject, so important to our honour, our condition, and our religion, demands the most solemn and effectual inquiry ; and I call upon your Lordships, and the united powers of the State, to examine it thoroughly and decisively, and to stamp upon it the indelible stigma of the public abhorrence. And I again implore those holy prelates of our religion to do away with these iniquities from among us. Let them perform a lustration ! Let them purify this House, and this country, from this sin !"

But alas ! among the hereditary counsellors, the bishops too sit silent and unmoved when those Acts of 1866 and 1869 were passed, which shook the bulwarks of our constitution, and which, pronouncing *that* to be a necessity which God has pronounced to be deadly sin, exalted its practice henceforth into an acknowledged and regulated traffic !

CHAPTER V.

THE offences which are punished under other Acts of Parliament, or according to the common law of England, are all either carefully defined by these Acts and that law, or else they are such as unmistakably to define themselves. In these Contagious Diseases Acts, on the contrary, there is no definition of the offence treated under them, nor do we find that the offence is such as unmistakably to define itself. On the contrary, we find amongst the advocates of these Acts, no less than in society generally, the widest possible variety of opinion as to the definition of a prostitute. This variety of opinion is only indicative of the immense difficulty of drawing any marked line as to where a woman may be justly designated by this name. There are many easy-going persons of the upper classes who know nothing of the poor, and who talk of this unhappy class as if they were as easily distinguishable as a negro is from a white man; but those who are acquainted with the poorer classes of women know the utter fallacy of this method of judgment, and are well aware that there is amongst this class of sinners as long and varied a series as in any other. Moreover, those who have looked at all carefully into the subject observe, that there are in human nature deeply-seated causes why this indistinctness of definition is maintained rather than otherwise; for they can scarcely help being conscious that the real cause of the difficulty which men who legislate on this subject experience in arriving at a just determination of that degree of guilt which is to attach this terrible appellation to a woman, arises in a great measure from the disingenuousness of men, and their disinclination that their sex should be acknowledged as the accomplices and companions of the persons thus defined. Until war be waged against impure men, as well as against impure women, it will remain impossible to define prostitution. It is amazing to see in this unequal war waged against the weaker sex only, how men who legislate for their own interests have, as it were, talked themselves into the notion, if it were possible to do so, that these poor women are sinners in this respect in their own single persons, and that male persons have no part whatever in the offence.

· The attempt to define a prostitute is as difficult as it is, in the long gradation of character among men, from the most virtuous to the most vicious, to fix on that point at which a man may be stamped as an

immoral character.   Nevertheless, if the purification
of society were the object of these laws, instead of the
protection of one sex against the other, it would be
possible, for legal purposes, to define prostitution, although the definition might be arbitrary.   But for the
purposes of this law, which does not aim at the purification of society, but only at the protection of one sex
against the other, it is absolutely necessary that definitions should be avoided, and that the wholesale treatment of the weaker sex should be carried on in a maze
of indefiniteness and arbitrary selection.

But without inquiry further into the causes which
operate to bring about this result, it is evident that
in the absence of any unanimity of opinion in the public
mind as to what constitutes a prostitute, and in presence of the difficulty of drawing the line which public
opinion admits, these Acts were bound to supply the
definition.   In the long line of women, extending from
the most virtuous to the most vicious, there are two
points at which the Acts might, if they pleased, have
defined prostitution.   Yet they adopt neither of these
definitions.   In the first place, they might have said
that every woman is to be called a prostitute under
these Acts who voluntarily and by some avowed method
assumes the name ; or secondly, that every woman who
is found associating, under any circumstances, with a

man, and who cannot produce a certificate of her marriage with him, is to be called a prostitute under the Acts.

Public opinion would not sanction the latter definition.

They did not adopt the former definition because it would not have been sufficiently inclusive for the purposes of the Act.

What they have really done is to leave the word undefined, and professing to adopt something like the former definition, thus soothing the alarms of justly-minded persons, they practically adopt the latter definition, with such arbitrary omissions as shall, in various places and at various times, seem good to the policeman of the district and the justice of peace of the district.[1]

The fact, indeed, which constitutes one of the greatest and most insidious practical abominations in connection with these Acts is the fact that, in virtue of this

---

[1] If they had adopted the former definition without reserving this power of arbitrary omission, this law would have told too heavily upon the great; but even supposing that virtue might have continued to wink even under this law, still oblivious to them, and might have continued, as doubtless it would, to regard that as pardonable frailty in high life which is called prostitution among the humbler classes, yet there are others who, under this law, might have been too conveniently assailed; for policemen, examining surgeons, nay even sometimes justices of the peace, may not be unacquainted with temporary connections with that mistress, their appreciation of whose faithfulness makes them dread for her the severity of such a definition.

non-definition of a prostitute, the policeman and justice
of the peace ride rampant at their pleasure throughout
all that immense border land of humble society which
lies between the confessed prostitute and absolute
virtue. All the objections which we have urged against
these Acts, with respect to the unconstitutional method
by which they decide whether a woman is a prostitute
or not, are intensified tenfold by the absence from the
Acts of any definition as to what constitutes prostitution. A justice of the peace is therefore set to decide
the question of fact as to a woman's character, in which
decision there are involved, as we have shown, most
grievous consequences; and he is set to do this with
absolutely no guide as to what is the thing which he is
to determine the woman to be or not to be,—no guide
either from the Acts in question, or from the concur-
rent unanimity of society at large. The result of this
is, and must be, that the definition of what a prostitute
is, gradually falls into the hands of the policeman who
accuses her; a grievous and lamentable consequence of
this law, which constitutes one of its greatest oppressions, whereby the whole operation of the law degener-
ates into a mere hunting in the streets by policemen
of women suspected by them of unchastity.

In all offences which are punished by law, and which
are capable of graduation, as all offences are, there is

established a corresponding graduation of punishment, which usually varies through very wide limits.

Under the Acts in question there is no graduation of punishment, although, as we have seen, there is such a graduation of offence that the law cannot even define where the offence begins. The same punishment is meted to all, and the same treatment. It may be necessary for the purposes of this Act that it should be so. If it is thus necessary, the Act again stands condemned by this very admission. Let the reader compare this law then with any other summary case, for instance that of petty theft. If a man steal, theft is defined exactly, and the case is submitted to the justice, who, taking into account all the circumstances of temptation, of youth, or of poverty, administers a punishment such as he may think commensurate to the particular offence. Here an offence distinctly defined is submitted to a justice, who selects a commensurate punishment.

But in the case under this Act it is exactly the reverse. It is the punishment alone which is defined, and the definition of the offence is left to the justice.

There cannot be imagined a greater opportunity for error, nor a more utter reversal of all the principles of justice.

To submit such a case even to the superior tribunal of twelve selected men, in whose election the prisoner has a choice, would, under these circumstances of indefiniteness of charge, by no means secure for the accused a just decision. How much less is this likely to be secured under the circumstances of trial prescribed by the Act?

Let the reader observe too, in passing, the oppressive character of the Act. The Court is to be closed, unless the woman desires it to be open; it will generally be painful to the justice that such a case should be tried with open court. The first action of the law then is to bring the woman into opposition with that judge who not only, alone, is to determine the facts on which she is tried, but is also alone to define the offence.[1]

It may be said by some that should the woman be falsely condemned there is open to her the means of redress prescribed in this as in all similar Acts of Parliament. She may sue those concerned for damages, which she will get if she can prove that she has suffered an injury. I will not refer here to the great difficulties thrown in the way of any woman under these Acts obtaining any redress by the special clauses which refer to that redress. But it would seem as if the whole

---

[1] This appearance before the justice is only in case of disobedience to the Acts. In the first and all-important process of determining whether the woman be moral or vicious, not 10 per cent. of the women ever see the face of their judge, who condemns them on the hearsay evidence of the spy alone!

Act had been so framed that whereas errors under it should be inevitable, redress should be impossible. For if she be wrongly condemned for being a prostitute, how can she get redress for that false condemnation for an offence the definition of which is absolutely and entirely in the hands of the person who condemned her?

There is an infinite number of minor oppressions and necessary illegalities growing out of a law which is itself essentially oppressive and illegal, such as the intimidation by police, bribery, perpetual spying and eaves-dropping, the investing of the hospital surgeons with the powers of magistrate and gaoler in one, and illegal orders, in contravention even of the Acts themselves, issued by the War Office and the Admiralty, such as we have already referred to. On these, which are the vicious fruits of a vicious principle, it is not my object here to dwell; but there is one point to which, before leaving this part of the subject, I wish to call the reader's attention.

Clause 28, Act 1866, runs as follows:—"If any woman, subjected by an order of a justice under this Act to periodical medical examination, at any time temporarily absents herself in order to avoid submitting herself to such an examination, on any occasion on which she ought so to submit herself, or refuses or wilfully neglects to submit herself to such examination on

G

any such occasion; if any woman authorized by this Act to be detained in a certified hospital for medical treatment quits the hospital without being discharged therefrom by the chief medical officer thereof by writing under his hand (the proof of which shall lie on the accused); if any woman, authorized by this Act to be detained in a certified hospital for medical treatment, or any woman being in a certified hospital for medical treatment, for a contagious disease, refuses, or wilfully neglects, while in the hospital, to conform to the regulations thereof approved under this Act, then, and in every such case, such woman shall be guilty of an offence against this Act, and, on summary conviction, shall be liable to imprisonment, with or without hard labour, in the case of a first offence, for any term not exceeding one month; and, in the case of a second or any subsequent offence, for any term not exceeding three months; and in the case of the offence of quitting the hospital without being discharged as aforesaid, the woman may be taken into custody, without warrant, by any constable."

Clause 29, Act 1866 :—" If any woman is convicted of, and imprisoned for the offence of absenting herself, or of refusing or neglecting to submit herself to examination as aforesaid, the order subjecting her to periodical medical examination shall be in force after, and notwithstanding her imprisonment, unless the surgeon or other medical officer of the prison, or a visiting surgeon appointed under this Act, at the time of her discharge from imprisonment, certifies in writing to the effect that she is then free from a contagious disease (the proof of which certificate shall lie on her); and in that case the order subjecting her to periodical medical examination shall, on her discharge from imprisonment, cease to operate."

A woman, then, the question of whose honour has been determined by an illegal method of trial, and who has in consequence been adjudged to undergo these examinations, is, if she refuses to submit to them, sent to prison, at the end of which time, when she is let out of prison, she may find the order for her examination still in full force. If she again refuses, she must again go to prison. The option is continually given her, at each time she comes out, of submitting to this examination fortnightly for a year, or of again going back to prison.

This part of the law alone is more worthy of the Spanish Inquisition than of this free country. There never was a law so calculated at every point to be the vehicle of persecution; and this iniquitous procedure is calculated to break the spirit of any woman. Such a law, such a mode of punishment—close imprisonment

for life, with the constantly presented alternative of a
brutal personal violation—such a punishment would
be bad enough if following after the most regular, constitutional, and careful trial and conviction. But what,
in God's name, are we to think of it when it follows on
a conviction such as I have already described ? That
these consequences may not be likely to happen is no
satisfactory answer; that it should be possible for them
to happen under the laws of England is itself sufficiently intolerable.

The whole treatment of the women who are brought
under the operation of these Acts has the general
character of those inquisitorial proceedings in the dark
ages, which are condemned by all, and the very record of
which is scarcely now permitted to be revived in any
publication.   There are cases of the ancient "peines
fortes et dures," which certainly did not involve bodily
pain, which latter was often preferred by the victims
when a choice was given. The inquisitors knew that
to wound the emotional part of a woman's nature was
oftentimes greater torture than actual laceration.[1]

[1] So anxious has our Legislature ever been to establish mercy
even to convicted offenders, as a fundamental principle of government, that they made it an express article of that great public
compact framed at the era of the Revolution—the Bill of Rights—
that " no cruel and *unusual* punishments" should ever be enforced
(see Bill of Rights, art. x.). They even added a clause for that
purpose to the oath which kings and queens were thenceforward to

In concluding this chapter, I cannot avoid this opportunity of saying, that although we have been as yet objecting to these Acts on account chiefly of the innocent, or comparatively innocent, yet we must strongly assert that, in the application of them to the most deeply guilty of the class of women who come under their operation, they are equally dangerous and reprehensible. For this reason, that the essential danger,

take at their coronation, thus endeavouring to render it an everlasting obligation to English monarchs to make justice "to be executed with mercy." In the same spirit they availed themselves, not only of the crisis of the Revolution, but of every important occasion, to procure new confirmations to be given to the right of trial by jury, and in general to the purity and integrity of our system of criminal jurisprudence. A curious debate took place in Parliament in 1605 (see Parliamentary Hist., vol. v.) on a proposal to introduce some unusual form of punishment for certain criminals. The motion was very speedily rejected. I find in some ancient books on law, that even in the execution of the "peines fortes et dures," regard was to be had to *decency*. A harrowing narrative of bodily pains, inflicted in order to urge the victim to confession, ends with the injunction to stop short of personal indecency towards him or her ; this last agony was seldom inflicted, and only under the most oppressive tyranny, and by a cruel and shameless executive. It is impossible to dwell further on this subject ; nor can one read such records without a burning shame on account of the degeneracy in this particular of our own times. It will be a sad day for Her Majesty when she wakes up to the full knowledge of the fact that she—a woman, a gracious and virtuous woman—has signed away with her own hand the liberties of a vast multitude of her subjects in a more complete fashion than has been attempted since the days of the Stuarts, and that she has unwittingly sanctioned deeds which make the heart of womanhood to freeze with horror.

which we have all along pointed out, lies in the infringement in any case whatsoever of our ancient mode of justice—an element of license introduced into our criminal code being the first step towards the extinction of liberty for all. When Parliament ventured in the last century to infringe upon the principles of our constitution, in the case of Mr. Wilkes,[1] Lord Chatham, in deprecating their action, spoke the following words: " The character of Mr. Wilkes has very improperly been introduced into this question ; for my own part, I consider him merely and indifferently as an English subject, possessed of certain rights which the laws have given him. In *his* person, though he were the *worst* of men, *I contend for the safety and security of the best ; and God forbid, my Lords, that there should ever be a power in this country of measuring the civil rights of the subject by his moral character, or by any other rule than the fixed law of the land.*"

Yet, strange to say, we find people whose ignorance is inexcusable, speaking as if some laxity in the matter of criminal justice towards this particular class of persons were of little consequence, since they are judged by common consent to be in a manner beyond the pale of society. Yet surely a man who has murdered some half-dozen persons, after the manner of William Palmer,

[1] Trial of John Wilkes, A.D. 1763.

may be equally considered as beyond the pale of society; yet in this case, and all similar cases, every possible precaution is taken in the matter of his trial ; and the character alike of our laws, and of those who dispense them, is felt to be involved in the justice of the verdict given. Such are the necessary and proper advantages granted by our laws to the most deeply dyed criminal who happens to be of the male sex. It points to something radically wrong, both in human nature and in our society, when the mere accident of the criminals being in this case women makes it possible for such illogical and loose notions to prevail in regard to what legal justice owes them. Again, let us call the reader's attention to the fact, that no amount of heinousness in the nature of those offences with which any class of the community may be charged, ought to deprive that class of the due exercise of impartial justice in regard to them. The creation of a proletariate class in a nation insures that nation eventually being smothered in its own mud.

I shall conclude this portion of my subject by drawing attention to the following exhaustive passage from Lieber, descriptive of the characteristics of a just form of criminal trial, and to the contrast which it presents in every particular to the laws which we condemn.

" Among the points which characterize," says Lieber,[1] " a fair, just, and sound penal trial, according to our advancement in political civilisation, we would designate the following :—No intimidation before the trial, or attempts by artifice to induce the prisoner to confess—a contrivance which protects the citizen even against being placed so easily in a state of accusation ;[2] the fullest possible realization of that principle, that every man is held innocent until proved to be otherwise ; bail ; a total discarding of the principle, that the more heinous the imputed crime is, the less ought to be the protection of the prisoner, but, on the contrary, the adoption of the reverse ; a distinct indictment, and the acquaintance of the prisoner with it sufficiently long before the trial to give him time for preparing the defence ; the accusatorial process, with jury and publicity, therefore an oral trial, and not a process in writing ; counsel or defensors for the prisoner ; a distinct theory of evidence, and no hearsay testimony ; a verdict upon evidence alone, in pronouncing guilty or not guilty ; a punishment in proportion to the offence,

[1] Lieber, vol. i. p. 56.

[2] " Trial itself," says Lieber (vol. i. p. 182), " though followed by acquittal, is a hardship." It is a peculiar hardship in the case of an accusation against a woman's honour, which, even where satisfactorily disproved, generally imposes a greater or less social stigma on the person falsely accused. Yet this disproval is all but impossible.

and in accordance with common sense and justice; especially, no punitory imprisonment, which must necessarily make the prisoner worse than he was when he fell into the hands of Government,[1] nor cautionary imprisonment before trial, which by contamination must advance the prisoner in his criminality;[2] that the punishment adapt itself as much as possible to the crime and criminality of the offender; that nothing but what the law demands or allows be inflicted, and that all the law demands be inflicted—no arbitrary injudicious pardoning,[3] which is a direct interference with the government by law."

[1] The imprisonment inflicted under clause 28, Act 1864, falls upon those women who have any spark of modesty or virtue left, and may drive it out of them.

[2] Compare this with the indiscriminate herding together of the women under the Acts in the examining-house.

[3] Poor women in the subjected districts have said to me: " *Pretty* girls get off far more easily than plain ones."

CHAPTER VI.

HAVING now pointed out the principal illegalities and oppressions which are the necessary results of a principle so evil as that which is embodied in the Acts to which we object, I shall point out two great evils, which are not yet fully appreciated, even by the most earnest opponents of the Acts.

It may be stated generally, that the very existence of these laws in any portion of the country gradually educates the nation to political incapacity and to moral obliquity, evils so vast and so insidious, as, by spreading like a plague-spot through the whole nation, to involve it eventually in national downfall.

I. It is already plainly perceived by many that the educational influence of these Acts is subversive of individual purity and private morality. It has not been so plainly perceived, however, that that influence is equally subversive of the balance of the social system, of the power of self-government, and of the due relations to each other of the different parts of the body politic, which hitherto have so largely contributed to the manliness of our national character.

Sir Edward Creasy says,[1] "It has been our happiness in England to combine the system of local distribution of power in matters of local importance with the system of centralization of power in matters of imperial policy. The practice of our nation for centuries establishes the rule that except for matters clearly of direct, general, and imperial interest, centralization is unconstitutional. I dwell on this topic, because during the last few years the principle of local self-government has been menaced, if not impaired, and because hasty and unreflecting observers can hardly have appreciated its national importance."

"We shall find," he continues,[2] "in local self-government infinitely more force than centralization ever could produce; we shall find that force to be far more general in its operation; and we shall find it far more enduring and certain, because it springs, not from the accidental idiosyncrasy of an individual ruler, but from the national spirit, and from the ancestral habits of a whole people. We ought to reflect also upon the pernicious indirect effects which centralization produces in a State, and on the advantages which we as a nation

[1] *English Constitution*, p. 372.   [2] *Ibid.* p. 374.

derive from being self-trained and locally practised in
the discharge of political duties. We should listen to
the testimony of intelligent foreigners, of men who have
lived under a plausible administrative hierarchy, and
who speak feelingly as to its effects."

The great French statesman De Tocqueville devotes
a chapter to the distinction between centralization in
matters of imperial government and centralization in
administrative matters of local interest; and while he
shows the necessity of the first, he demonstrates the
pernicious effects of the second, notwithstanding its
specious appearances. It is scarcely necessary to re-
mark that the Contagious Diseases Acts belong distinctly to that class of interests the imperial control of
which he so strongly reprobates.

Professor Lieber, a German by birth, but an American
by adoption, after describing the principles of the
American Congress and the English Parliament as free
institutions, expressly states, " Yet the self-government
of our country, or of England, could be considered by us
as little more than oil floating on the surface of the
water, did it consist only in Congress and the State
Legislatures with us (*i.e.*, in America), or in Parliament
in England. Self-government, to be of a penetrative
character, requires the institutional self-government of
the country or district; it requires that everything

which, without general inconvenience, can be left to the circle to which it belongs, be thus left to its own management."

The great German historian Niebuhr also, "before whose eyes the annals and institutions of almost every State, ancient or modern, were made to shed light on the annals and institutions of the rest,"—who was a man of practice and action, had spent part of his manhood in England, and had been employed in arduous undertakings for his own government, in a book on the *Internal Administration of Great Britain,*—edited in order, if possible, to induce his own government to reorganize their State on better principles, maintains that "British liberty depends at least as much on the local self-appliances of local governments, as it does upon Parliament."

" The self-governing spirit of our English system of internal polity," says Bowyer,[1] " explains that remarkable willingness to obey and even assist the law, which has sometimes excited the admiration of foreigners in this country."

M. Le Cour, the Chef-Administratif of the medical Police, who are employed in Paris for carrying out the laws in that city which are similar to the Contagious Diseases Acts, gives it as his opinion that " such

[1] *Commentaries,* p. 373.

Acts will work admirably in England, and will succeed there better than in Paris, owing to the habits of obedience to the law which are so universally diffused among the people of England," oblivious that the very system he wishes to graft upon this spirit of obedience, is that which contains in itself the seeds of the ruin of that spirit of obedience, and which strikes at the foundation of that very habit of local self-government to which this spirit of obedience is so universally referred.   Such is the political blindness of those who legislate for the necessity of prostitution.

In a treatise by the French statesman Count Montalembert, " On the Political Future of England," he forcibly exposes the evils which must ensue if there is any increase of administrative centralization, of what he terms " bureaucratie," in this country ; especially he shows its debasing influence on a nation in another matter, and warns us to reflect on the fact that the multiplication of salaried functionaries creates a population of place-hunters.   " An universal thirst," says he, " after salaried public employments is the worst of social maladies.   It infects the whole body politic with a venal and servile humour, which by no means excludes, even amongst those who may be the best paid, the spirit of faction and anarchy.   It creates a crowd of hungry suitors, capable of every excess to satisfy their

longings, and fit instruments for every base purpose as
soon as they are in place."

These general statements will commend themselves
to the minds of most English readers. Let them then
be fully awake to the dangers which are now undermining these cherished advantages of the system under
which we have, up till this time, lived. It is strange
that while a strong stand is being made at present for the
freer exercise of local self-government, and a practical
step in that direction has been taken in the extension
of the municipal franchise, a step, and a most fatal step,
has been taken in the opposite direction by the Government through the Acts which we condemn; and we
have already had exhibited to us as its fruits a sight
unwonted in England—the sight of an energetic Cor-
poration completely set aside and overruled within the
limits of its own jurisdiction by the creatures of imperial tyranny, the very lowest of the executive. This
is the first-fruits in England of the great and fatal effort
at centralization begun by these Acts.

Are the people of England willing, not only that
personal liberty should be interfered with, but that
corporate freedom should be threatened with annihila-
tion by these Acts of Parliament, which unless repealed
will no doubt be followed by others equally aggressive
in principle, against which we shall then have no argu-

ment,—a result which will, as we may learn from the words which we have just quoted, be little less than the destruction of the stability of English political life?

And this centralization, which is so much to be deprecated, is introduced by these Acts with those very concomitants which render its effect most ruinous, namely, the establishment of a system of police espionage, a thing utterly foreign and abhorrent to all the instincts and convictions of Englishmen. On the subject of that constant and minute police interference which these laws have introduced so extensively into England, I may quote the weighty words of Lieber.

"It is necessary," says he, in his *Political Ethics*, "to have seen nations who have been forced for centuries to submit to constant and minute police interference, in order to have any conception of the degree to which manly action, self-dependence, resoluteness, and inventiveness of proper means can be eradicated from a whole community. On this account systematic interference weakens governments instead of strengthening them; for in times of danger, when popular energy is necessary, when every man must do his duty, or the State is lost, men having forgotten how to act, look listlessly to the Government, not to themselves. The victories of Napoleon over the many States east and south of France were in a great measure owing to this natural course of things."

These words need no comment. But can we imagine any form of the evil here indicated more fit than that embodied in these Acts to produce the pernicious consequences described, and to lead men back from manhood into babyhood? For by these Acts it is implied that men are so helplessly the slaves of their own lower passions, so little in possession of the gift of self-control, so little fit to manage themselves, that they must needs be protected from the consequences of their own unnecessary vice, and taught to lean upon this great centralizing and protecting authority, in place of on the help of God and a resolute and manly will.

II. The Contagious Diseases Acts have been introduced into England solely on medical grounds. They have been argued for by their supporters solely on medical grounds, and every attempt has been continually made to restrict the question to a medical question. Yet the continual insistance of the opposition on the immoral tendencies of the Acts, and the generally evinced and growing determination of the country at large to treat the question as a moral question, and to regard that question as of primary importance in comparison with the medical question—all this has brought about a very significant change in the position taken up by the supporters of the Acts, who now attempt to make out that their tendencies are

H

highly moral, as perhaps they may endeavour, after reading the arguments advanced in this Essay, to make them out to be highly constitutional. They have openly boasted in and out of Parliament that more has been achieved by their salaried police and medical officers than has ever been accomplished by the unwearying efforts of Christian societies and independent workers, and that their achievements in the matter of spiritual influence and moral conversions have dwarfed all that has ever been recorded in the annals of Christian evangelization in this direction.[1] Similarly they will no doubt by and by show with equal success that the system which they have introduced is a bulwark of our constitutional liberties, in comparison of which Magna Charta, Habeas Corpus Act, and Jury Trial have been lamentable and conspicuous failures.

In the expectation of having this proved to us in

[1] See Dr. Lyon Playfair's speech in the House. See also Lane's pamphlet, p. 15. See also the Report of the Committee of the House of Commons, from which we make the following extract :—

"116. *Question*—Do you know of your own knowledge whether it is not the case that attempts to reform these women by approaching them with direct moral and religious advice, while they are pursuing their avocation, are generally unsuccessful? *Answer*—It is almost always inoperative.

"117. I suppose it has been attempted at Devonport by clergymen and others ?—Very constantly."

The effrontery of this statement is almost unparalleled when we consider the glorious but hitherto unappreciated achievements of the various Rescue Societies.

numerous pamphlets to the absolute satisfaction of the writers of the same, I cannot avoid this opportunity of investigating a little more closely the so-called moral arguments brought forward in favour of the Acts. In doing so I do not for a moment intend to return to that unprofitable dispute which they prolong regarding certain reclamations which they claim of a percentage of their patients in hospital. But I would call attention to the following fact, that our opponents always, and up to the present moment, in speaking of the " moral view," include in that expression only that wretchedly limited portion of the question which relates to the annual exodus from this degrading trade of a certain number of public women, an exodus which they who are acquainted with the circumstances of the lives of such women before the Acts ever came into existence, know to have been always going on to a very much greater extent than the upholders of these Acts take cognisance of. Whereas this has, without exception, been the limit of our opponents' view of the extent of the moral question involved, our view of that question has extended far beyond the moral influence of this legislation on the immediate victims of it, and has embraced its influence on the country at large, and that not only considered in its character as a direct encouragement to license, through the protection offered,

but also in its character as a warping and blinding
influence on the judgments and consciences of men of
all classes who may themselves not be guilty of any
personal impurity.   It is a most inadequate and narrow
view of the morality of which we speak as undermined
by the Acts, which is exclusively confined to sexual
morality.   Injustice is immoral; oppression is immoral;
the sacrifice of the interests of the weaker to the
stronger is immoral; and all these immoralities embodied in these iniquitous Acts, and continually contemplated, as they must be, by all that portion of the
nation who have no direct connection with the working
of them, are a demoralizing influence of the most deadly
character.

I cannot too much insist upon the weight which we
who oppose these Acts attach to the statement which
we have so frequently made, that they are calculated to
transfer the essential element of guilt from the vice to
the infringement of this law.   Under the action of this
law we maintain that gradually society at large comes
to regard as evil and good, not vice and virtue absolutely, but, vice not regulated by this law, and vice
regulated by this law.   Men's talk, inferences, actions
come to be all based upon a false distinction, the distinction between regulated and unregulated vice, and

the true distinction between vice and virtue is lost
sight of.

A Report as to the operation of the Contagious Diseases
Acts has been recently issued and sanctioned by Government, which contains the following clause :—" The improvement that has taken place in the persons, clothing,
and homes of the common women as regards cleanli-
ness and order is most marked. Many of the women
formerly looked bloated from drink, whilst others were
greatly emaciated and looked haggard through disease.
Their language and habits are greatly altered—swearing, drunkenness, and indecency of behaviour have
become quite exceptional; the women now look fresh
and healthy, and are most respectful in their manner ;
in fact, these poor creatures feel that they are not
altogether outcasts from society, but that there are
people who still take an interest in their moral and
physical welfare."

If the Report is to be regarded as a mere statement
of fact, we who object to these laws on moral grounds
could find no stronger argument than these words to
prove the tendency of the law to extend the practice of
fornication among men. The tone of satisfaction, however, with which the framer of the Report evidently
dwells on this result of the Acts, cannot but be felt to
be, to a certain extent, a verification of what I have

said about submission to these Acts usurping the place of virtue in public opinion. But the full force of that statement is verified very terribly when we find a supporter[1] of these Acts quoting this sentence, with the words, " the women now look fresh and healthy," in italics, as the crowning moral benefit conferred on society by the Acts.

I would observe here that the writer of the Report has taken refuge in an expression calculated to mislead hasty readers. He uses the word " the women" in a sense in which our opponents are peculiarly fond of using it. I wish simply to challenge the writer of this Report to show his meaning more clearly by asking him this simple question : To what women do you refer when you boast of their moral and physical improvement ? Clearly not to those women who are escaping, or have escaped, from the toils of sin ; because the moment they begin thus to escape, they are removed from your supervision and cognisance, they return to virtuous life, or seek the privacy of the Refuge, and henceforward cease to be objects of interest to you in the matter of the clearness of their complexion or the amiability of their manners. Who, then, I ask again, are the women of whose moral and physical improvement you boast ? I will answer for you ; and now let us read this sentence

[1] Lane's answer to Duncan M'Laren.

again with the proper and honest word substituted in the place of " the women :"—

" *The harlots* now look fresh and healthy, and are most respectful in their manner."

We find in the report of the Committee of the House of Commons, which sat on these Acts, and recommended their recent extension, the following piece of evidence :—

" 592. There was one house into which I went with the inspector of police lately. I heard a woman reading with a loud voice. When we got in the passage I stopped to listen, and I found, to my astonishment, that she was reading from Bunyan's *Pilgrim's Progress.* I went into the room and found no less than seven women sitting round a good-looking female of twenty-five, who was reading from the Pilgrim's Progress, all paying the greatest attention.

"593. Was the woman reading it in a spirit which showed that she was feeling what she was reading?— Most decidedly; I never saw clergyman or audience in a church look more serious than the reader or the listeners.

" 594. Were those prostitutes ?—They were.

" 595. Were they engaged in the prosecution of their trade ?—Most decidedly ; I have, I am sorry to say, two or three of them in the hospital now."

The reader will observe, however, that in this instance the witness whose moral obliquity was such that he could suppose that his evidence evinced a moral improvement in the character of a harlot, was probably an uneducated Government official; but now we find the framers of Government reports, and advocates of this Act in high place, falling into exactly the same confusion, and mistaking obedience to this Act for moral rectitude.

We deeply deplore this deadly confusion, which we maintain that these Acts give rise to, and believe it to be fraught with the most ruinous moral consequences to England, bringing, as it must, in its train moral obliquity and the spread of fornication. We further maintain that that moral obliquity is here introduced at a point in social relationship where its introduction is more calculated than at any other to undermine the whole moral code of the country. Striking at the root of family life by the encouragement of prostitution, it introduces a complete confusion of right and wrong, with respect to a vice more typical than any other, and is calculated to reproduce itself in moral enormities through the whole fabric of social life.

But what moral enormity can surprise us now, when we have found that the Admiralty and the War Office have risen up to be the saviours of the souls of women?

I might address them in the words in which Milton once addressed the Treasury Bench :—" Indeed, my Lords of the Admiralty and the War Office, are ye at last become the gracious guardians of those principles which in your hearts you despise ? Or has the Spirit at length beamed in light upon souls where light never shone before ? For shame, my Lords ! will ye never forsake inconsistance ? Demons have trembled and Jews have been converted, but when the cause of religion is echoed from the Admiralty and War Office, perfidy is at hand, and we ought to look about us."[1]

[1] Preface to the *Areopagitica.*

CHAPTER VII.

I HAVE before alluded to the two great struggles in the history of this country, which, occasioned by the arbitrary encroachments of those in power, led to the more sure establishment of our constitutional privileges. These revolutions and their results, which have been the wonder and admiration of all foreign writers, owing to their success, and the sober and resolute method in which they were conducted, were chiefly brought about through the union of all classes in opposition to these encroachments,—a union not marred by selfish and party interests. These great struggles are worthy of the deep and earnest contemplation of every English man and woman who cares for the welfare of our country, and who, conscious of the ever-recurring tendency in human nature to spoliation and aggression, is sternly jealous of the rights and blessings purchased by the efforts and by the blood of our forefathers. Alarmed again in our own day by the insidious advances of despotic power in the midst of us, and convinced that what is morally wrong can never be politically right, they will turn an earnest and searching gaze upon these records of the past, and in doing so cannot fail to be stimulated to hold fast and contend for, even to death if need be, those blessings which were so hardly and so nobly won. The battle which we have now to fight is in its essential character the same as those which resulted formerly in confirmations of our liberties, and in a firmer establishment of a just and virtuous state. The principles arrayed on either side in this conflict are essentially the same as those which inspired the combatants of the past. Great constitutional rights have ever been vindicated by those out of power against the encroachments of those in power; but the scene of the battle is changed. It is not now the Barons arrayed against the King, nor the insulted Commons against the Court party, and the aggressions of favourites in power. The tyranny which we are now opposing has sprung up in a quarter which in the era of the English Revolution could scarcely have been suspected as likely ever to become dangerous. Our present peril arises from the arbitrary disposition of permanent officers of the Government, aided by the blindness of Her Majesty's ministers, and the contempt for, or ignorance of, our ancient constitutional rights which prevails among a proportion of the members of both of our Houses of Parliament. The power of

the Crown, almost dead and rotten as prerogative, has
grown up anew with far more strength in a new quarter,
which, still possessing the confidence of the people,
makes the exercise of that arbitrary power doubly
dangerous. The painful discovery has been made that
the forms of a free government and the ends of an arbitrary government are not incompatible. The evil principles at work in this piece of legislation to which we
are opposed, went craftily, and too successfully, to work,
and the conduct of the promoters of these laws may be
described in the following words of Mr. Burke :[1]—

" They who will not conform their conduct to the
public good, and cannot now support it by the prerogative of the Crown, have adopted a new plan—they have
totally abandoned the shattered and old-fashioned
fortress of prerogative, and made a lodgement in the
stronghold of Parliament itself. If they have any evil
design to which there is no ordinary legal power commensurate, they bring it into Parliament ; in Parliament
the whole is executed from the beginning to the end ; in
Parliament the power of obtaining their object is absolute, and the safety of the proceeding perfect—no rules
to confine, no after reckonings to terrify.[2] Parliament

[1] " Thoughts on the Cause of the Present Discontents."—Burke's
Works, p. 140.

[2] With these considerations in their mind, I can conceive how safe
and comfortable the fathers of the Contagious Diseases Acts felt

cannot with any great propriety punish others for things in which they themselves have been accomplices. Thus the control of Parliament upon the executive power is lost, and impeachment, that great guardian of the purity of the constitution, is in danger of being lost even to the very idea of it."

It must be confessed that the representatives of the people have been false to the people in allowing this surrender of the rights and liberties of any portion of them to be made in secret, and with that stealthy swiftness too clearly indicative of the fears of those who dared so to legislate. Ignorance and absence from the House have been pleaded by many members of Parliament as an excuse for their virtual complicity in this legislation. Their crime against the Constitution may be less than that of those who framed and watched over this legislation, but ignorance may not, any more than presumption, occupy the seat of our lawgivers.[1]

themselves—no visions of a future possible repeal of this Act to trouble them !

[1] "I am very much afraid," says a member of Parliament in a recent letter, "that one cause of our weakness in fighting this battle in the House is, that there are too many of its members who secretly like these Acts, as making, as they think, their own immoralities less personally dangerous to them ; there are many most excellent men on both sides, but I am afraid there are also many on whom wealth and station have had an injurious effect, who spend their lives merely for pleasure, and care nothing for higher considerations. This may seem strong language, but it is, I fear, too true."

Nevertheless our conviction is, that we shall ere long be able to reckon the Commons once more, as in times past, on the side of right and of constitutional freedom, as opposed to despotism; for we have this trust, that the Commons of England will yet be found faithful, and that the people's representatives will once more prove themselves the champions and the guardians of our liberties and of our national honour. Were it not for this hope, were it not for the inestimable blessing of a comparatively pure representative system of government, and still more, were it not for our conviction of the love of virtue, freedom, and justice which lives and burns in the great heart of England's humbler classes, to guide and inspire their representatives, our hearts might die within us as we contemplate the spectacle of the growing infidelity in high places to vital principles, and the audacious attempts to undermine our Constitution, for which attempts, if ignorance be the excuse, our case would be equally deplorable. Yet in spite of ignorance, infidelity, or selfish passion on the part of our rulers, we nevertheless retain that faith in the vigour and purity of English representative government which is breathed in the following noble words of De Lolme :[1]—

"How long soever the people may have remained in a state of supineness as to their most valuable interests,

[1] *English Constitution.*

whatever may have been the neglect and even the errors of their representatives, the instant the latter come either to see these errors or to have a sense of their duty, they proceed by means of the privileges we have mentioned to abolish those abuses or practices which during the preceding years had taken the place of the laws. To how low soever a state public liberty may happen to be reduced, they take it where they find it, lead it back through the same path and to the same point from which it had been compelled to retreat; and the ruling power, whatever its usurpations may have been, how far soever it may have overflowed its banks, is ever brought back to its old limits."

The continuance up to this time of the encroachments made on the Constitution by these Acts which we oppose, may perhaps be accounted for by the fact that the class of persons first assailed were those with whom society has in general the least sympathy; whereas in similar crises of danger in past times our liberties were violated in the person or persons generally of men of rank, influence, or high character. Nevertheless, this was not always the case, for, as Blackstone says, it was the injury done to a common citizen (one Jenks) which gave existence to the Act which completed the security of public liberties; "the oppression of an obscure individual gave rise to the

famous Habeas Corpus Act." Junius has observed that
this is worthy of note, for the just idea it conveys of
that readiness of all orders of men in England to unite
in defence of common liberty. I am convinced that
Englishmen now are not so degenerate as not to contend with equal zeal for the redress of wrongs which
are no less dangerous because inflicted on a class whom
society generally despises, or upon those the humble-
ness of whose position or whose unsheltered fame
leaves it possible for men carelessly to confuse them
with the guilty. This encroachment on our liberties
has come upon us "like a lion and wolf in one,"
rapacious and devouring, but sly and soft-footed. Had
our ancient and dearly loved constitutional freedom
been attacked in a more open manner, had the first
sufferers been persons accustomed to demand and to
receive justice, the evil would have been quickly
averted, so loud and instantaneous would have been
the outcry; but because this lion-wolf set its paw first
upon the meanest of England's citizens, the danger is
but the greater. The gallant ship of our Constitution
may be as fatally wrecked by the falling of some
unseen spark in the remotest, dingiest corner of its
hold, as by the flash of lightning which strikes the
headmast in the sight of all, and sends it through the
waters a perishing mass of flames. "The Hollander in

the midst of the storm, though trusting to the strength
of the mounds that protect him, shudders no doubt at
the sight of the foaming element that surrounds him;
but they all give themselves over for lost when they
know that the worm has penetrated into their dykes."[1]
" The floods of ungodliness have made me afraid," says
the Psalmist, but we may have even greater reason to
fear when the element which is to destroy filters up
from beneath.　I have pondered the mournful saying
of Montesquieu, " Have not Rome, Lacedæmon, and
Carthage perished ?　So will this beautiful system of
the English Constitution perish when the legislative
power shall have become more corrupt than the executive."　And I ask myself with sorrow, " Can it be that
my country has already begun to tread this downward
path ?"　Doubtless when the Legislature has acted the
part of a traitor in surrendering the dearest and most
ancient rights of any portion of the nation into the
hands of the executive, whose power it has ever been
the wisdom of our laws to restrain within the strictest
limits, it may be said that the legislative power has
become more corrupt than that executive which is itself
on the highway to corruption through this very cession
into its hands of functions which it never ought to
exercise.

[1] De Lolme.

I

"Self-government," Grattan truly said, "is life." But
it is so in the fullest sense only when those who govern
themselves, having a voice in the making of the laws
which they themselves obey, possess that life of the
spirit and that enlightenment of conscience which is
nourished in the purity of honourable homes and by the
study of the Word of God. And who shall say that
there is not still such life in England? The present
crisis will test the life which there is in us; it will gauge
the moral condition of our people. If it find them
degenerated from the manly stature of their forefathers,
who were alike the champions of God's truth and of
human liberty, then we may well speak to them the
warning words of Rousseau, "Ye free nations, remember
this maxim, Freedom may be acquired, but it cannot be
recovered."[1] We have but partially and for a short
time lost that freedom; there is yet time to recover lost
ground, to turn back the tide of corruption and slavish-
ness[2] which will follow this false step. But the crisis
is grave, the necessity for action is urgent, and, if we
delay, the time for recovery will be passed; and

[1] Rousseau's *Social Contract*, chap. viii.

[2] "Such arbitrary courses have an ill operation upon the courage
of a nation, by embasing the hearts of the people. A servile condition does, for the most part, beget in men a slavish temper and disposition. Those that live so much under the whip and the pillory,
and such servile engines as were frequently used by the Earl of
Strafford, they may have the dregs of valour, sullenness, and stub-

henceforward we shall be given up, as other nations which we have seen, to the miserable alternations of raging fever and of death-like torpor, of revolution and of despotism.

But this "self-government which is life" has been despised by those holding a commission from the nation. Was this law against which we contend made by the nation ? Assuredly not. Nay, nor was it even made by Parliament, but by a mere fraction of Parliament casting off for a time the faith and responsibility of men commissioned by the nation. The people were not yet so degraded as to consent to such a law. Even where their education is but poor, the people nevertheless still know right from wrong ; they are yet able to distinguish between truth and falsehood, between freedom and slavery. It may be said of our industrial classes generally as Lord Chatham said of our forefathers who framed the Great Charter :—" Their virtues were rude and uncultivated, but they were great and sincere ; their understandings were as little polished as their manners, but they had hearts to distinguish right

bornness which may make them prone to mutinies and discontents. Shall it be treason to embase the king's coin, though but a piece of twelve pence, or six pence ? and must it not needs be the effect of a greater treason to embase the spirits of his subjects, and to set a stamp and character of servitude upon them whereby they shall be disabled to do anything for the service of the king and commonwealth ?"—Pym's Speech on the Trial of the Earl of Strafford, from wrong; they had heads to distinguish truth from falsehood; they understood the rights of humanity, and they had spirit to maintain them."

All the evils incident to our system of government arise when that government ceases at any period to be honestly representative of those masses of the people whose spirit we have described; and it is evident that when our rulers are swayed too much by any particular class in the community, they become no longer truly representative.

The narrower the class of persons exercising this undue influence, the greater is the danger; and that danger is heightened still further when this influence proceeds exclusively from men of one profession. The profession to which I now allude is the medical profession. I wish to guard myself against the suspicion of a general and unreasoning prejudice against this profession, which Guizot has styled "the mournfullest and the noblest." We have all of us too much reason to be grateful to men of that profession, many of whom we know by experience to be among the truest friends of humanity. But physicians who hang about courts, who have the ear of royalty, and of aristocratic public officers, and who exercise an influence over superstitious households of the great, somewhat resembling that formerly exercised by the priest in Italy and Spain, when allowed to influence our legislation in the direct manner which they have done of late, must be content to endure the searching judgment of the people at large, and ultimately to fall under the people's indignation, if they be found to be interfering with our laws, in defiance or in ignorance of the principles of our Constitution. Such medical men have not unfrequently risen to posts of honour, high among the aristocracy of the land, by an energy and talent which we cannot fail to admire.; but it cannot be denied that they frequently attain to excellence in the single line of professional study to which they have been necessarily devoted, at the expense of other portions of education essentially needful for those who would venture on meddling with the great and difficult science of governing. This deficiency is deeply dangerous in persons who have the hardihood to assume the responsibility of prompting the legislative measures of those who are bound to hold themselves accountable to the people alone. While observing the overwhelming influence which these professionals have lately been allowed in the making of laws for the whole nation, I have sometimes been appalled at the evidence which comes before us of their profound ignorance of English history, its noble struggles, the structure and resources of our political system, and the great constitutional principles

which we hold dear. They seem to have as little
appreciation of these matters as they have of the feelings and souls of human beings. Their ignorance both
of our political constitution, and of the principles which
animate human nature, are proved by their audacious
attempts at wholesale compulsion.[1] They scarcely
would have succeeded had they brought their present tactics to bear upon a nation barely emerg-
ing from childhood, and accustomed to obey the rule
of a despotic monarch. How dangerous is their
attempt when made upon a people to whom constitutional freedom is dear, will be proved by the future

[1] In a letter to the *Lancet*, a gentleman signing himself Stanley
Haynes, M.D., suggests that the Government should erect vast
establishments, to which " all persons ill with scarlatina, measles,
roseola, variola, varicella, relapsing fever, typhus, enteric, or yellow
fevers, diphtheria, pertussis, or cholera," should be conveyed in
spite of any remonstrances or resistance to the contrary ; such
establishments to be for all classes, and the removal of the patients
to be insisted on, " whenever the medical officer of health is satisfied that isolation and disinfection will not be complete at home,"
—even in this latter case the sick-rooms at home to be entered only
by persons authorized by an officer of health. The writer says that
this system " would be equal to the beneficial extension of the Contagious Diseases Acts to eruptive, continued, and mucous fevers."
He suggests that " much opposition would undoubtedly be roused
by parents and others," but that may be in time overcome, as the
opposition to the Contagious Diseases Acts is to be overcome, by
custom, and education to the system. This scheme, which reads
like a grim parody of the Contagious Diseases Acts, is indorsed
by the *Lancet*, which speaks of the " importance" of Dr. Haynes's
letter.
  In recent numbers of the *Lancet* there has been a correspond-

ruin of the influence of that whole class which has
attempted it. The limitations of their education produce a narrowness of intellect, which blinds them to
the limits of their own legitimate influence. Hence
the fatal mistake into which they have fallen. Compulsion is dear to them as life; the passion for compulsion grows by the indulgence granted to them by
our foolish legislators. Who can tell to what they will
compel us next? For their ignorance of history and of
human nature lead them to run riot in our political constitution, which they do not understand; they tell us
such and such questions are purely medical questions,
ence on the desirableness, from the doctor's point of view, of
making it compulsory on all women of the humbler classes, on
pain of fine or imprisonment, to be attended in childbearing by a
male practitioner. One of the correspondents says there is such a
provision in the new " Medical Bill," but on looking through that
Bill I cannot find such a provision, unless indeed it be artfully
concealed in clause 29. The *Lancet*, it is well known, is ever the
friend of compulsion and violent centralization, abounding in such
expressions as the following :—" It is to be regretted that a well
instructed and humane government does not exercise a firmer influence over the anarchy, the greed, the ignorance of local governing
bodies. But the energetic use of the powers given by the Sanitary
Acts would enable medical men to confer benefits on the public,
the value of which defies estimation."—*Lancet*. These benefits conferred by medical men, be it observed, are to be purchased at the
expense of that power of self-government, disposition to help the
law, and manly independence which, as we have seen, De Tocqueville, Montalembert, Niebuhr, Guizot, and a host of thoughtful
English writers, have attributed to a great extent to the freedom of
local governing bodies. It might be asked further, is there no
danger of anarchy, of greed, of ignorance among medical men ?

while they are secretly, through carelessness or ignorance, or consciously, robbing us like burglars in the night of our cherished inherited safeguards, dearer to us than wealth or health ; and by the arbitrary measures which they persuade a credulous or ignorant Legislature to adopt, by suspending the liberties of the citizen on all hands, and finally by abandoning the vital principle of jury trial in order that a project of theirs may work, they have at last taken that fatal step towards " establishing aristocracy, the most oppressive of absolute governments." And let the people of England never forget that the government of an aristocracy does not consist in that of wealth or hereditary privileges so much as in that arbitrary power of a particular class, whose enactments are permitted to override the safeguards of our Constitution.

I cannot sufficiently warn the people of England of the need of a jealous watchfulness over the actions of these law-making doctors. The Contagious Diseases Act of 1869 was smuggled through the House of Commons in three days; there is now another Bill emanating from the same source which will probably shortly come also before the House, some of the provisions of which (already alluded to in a note) may be found to be of a character as oppressive though not so immoral as those which I have been describing. It behoves the people of England, therefore, narrowly to watch, lest, through the collusion of doctors and aristocratic law-makers, the liberties of the free citizens of England should be even further and more grievously infringed than they already have been.

I have hitherto bestowed upon our Constitution unmitigated praise; but in the laws of England there is one great and unique defect. We can scarcely open the works of our great lawyers of past times without observing, that, even among those who most eulogize our system of laws, there is an uneasy consciousness of something somewhere wrong. At Liverpool, in the spring of 1870, a case was tried of a man of thirty years of age who had assaulted criminally a child of fourteen years, who had been an under-servant in his house. The defence set up was *consent.* "Mr. Justice Willes, in passing sentence, said he hoped that, in cases where girls between twelve and fourteen years of age were assaulted or seduced, the question as to their consent would attract public attention, and that largely; he had had to try a great many cases of this kind, especially where girls were servants, and where their masters, instead of protecting the poor children under their charge, had corrupted them; he hoped that what the Bishop of Winchester had so often attempted, though unsuccessfully,—to have the law which extended

only to twelve years of age extended to girls of fourteen,—would yet be accomplished, and that outrages
upon these little ones would be made an offence against
law without any question of consent. He felt very
deeply on this subject, and his experience showed him
the necessity of protection for girls of tender years; it
was quite absurd to suppose that a law which applied
to girls of twelve should not apply to girls of fourteen,
as girls were mere children up to fully the age of
fourteen."[1] The laws of most other countries make the
seduction of any woman under twenty-one a misdemeanour; but our laws, to the disgrace of Englishmen,
allow the seduction of any child over twelve. If a
villain can persuade the dispensers of the law that he
can show that there was consent on the part of the
child whom he ruined, he is free. [Acting upon this
rule, these Acts we are opposing take children of
twelve, and even younger, outrage them, bind them
over to return again and again to be outraged, and turn
them back upon the streets.] An eye-witness of the
trial alluded to remarked that pity and anger strove
together in her breast, as she looked at the poor little
creature, dwarfed both in body and mind, uneducated,
indigent, and exceedingly childish, standing shivering in
her ragged pinafore, to be judged as a "woman" who

[1] *Liverpool Mercury.*

had given the consent of a mature will to the immoral
act, and as she thought of the tenderness of the law to
the man—with all his advantages of age, education,
manner, position, money, and experience of life,—who
had ruined that child.

I have here indicated the weak point in English law.
The same want of justice appears in the law which, till
lately, made marriage the confiscation of all the wife's
earnings, and is further exhibited in the disgracefully
slight punishment inflicted for assaults on women and
children.[1]

Blackstone says,[2] "It is a remarkable omission in
the law of England which, with such scrupulous
solicitude, guards the rights of individuals, and secures
the morals and good order of the community, that
it should have afforded so little protection to female
chastity. It is true that it has defended it from
force and violence, but it has left it exposed to
perhaps greater danger from the artifices and solici-
tations of seduction. In no case whatsoever, unless
she has had a promise of marriage, can a woman

[1] If we compare the slight penalties inflicted for cruelties practised on women and children with those imposed for injury of
property or the wounding of a stag, the property of a Duke, we
cannot wonder at the low estimate, in England, of the worth of
women.

[2] *Commentaries*, p. 142, chap. viii.

herself obtain any reparation for the injury she has
sustained from the seducer of her virtue. And even
where her weakness and credulity have been imposed.
upon by the most solemn promises of marriage, unless
they have been overheard or made in writing, she cannot recover any compensation, being incapable of giving
evidence in her own cause. Nor can a parent maintain
any action against the person who has done this wrong
to his family, and to his honour and happiness, but by
stating and proving that, from the consequences of the
seduction, his daughter is less able to assist him as a
servant, or that the seducer was a trespasser on his
premises. Hence no action can be maintained which
is not attended with the loss of service or an injury to
property. Therefore in that action for seduction which
is in most general use, the father must prove that his
daughter actually assisted in some degree, however inconsiderable, in the housewifery of his family, and that
she has been rendered less serviceable to him by her
pregnancy; or the action might be sustained upon the
evidence of a consumption or any other disorder con-
tracted by the daughter in consequence of her seduction,
or of her shame and sorrow for the loss of her honour.
It is immaterial what is the age of the girl; but it is
necessary that she should be living in and considered
part of her father's family. Another action for seduc-

tion is a common action for trespass, which may be brought when the seducer has illegally entered the father's house; in which action the debauching his daughter may be stated as an aggravation of the trespass. But these are the only actions which have been extended, by the modern ingenuity of the courts, to enable an unhappy parent to recover a recompense for the injury he has sustained by the seduction of his daughter."

I feel sure that the hearts of fathers and mothers among the working classes of England will respond, when I speak of the gross influence and teaching of such a state of the law as this, and of the low estimate of the worth of female honour which alone could have induced it. Here we see that the property of the father, and the material usefulness of his daughter in the house, are set above all the claims of female honour, and above all the considerations of family affection. It is true of nations as well as of individuals, "whatsoever a man soweth that shall he also reap." We see in all the horrors which our Police Courts at this day reveal to us, of brutality towards women, of heartlessness and treachery in men of the upper classes towards the daughters of the poor, and in the levity and coarseness which accompany the exposure of these villanies, the disgusting and terrible fruits of this one corrupt seed of selfishness and injustice which, for so many generations past, has been marring the beauty of our English laws.[1]

The Contagious Diseases Acts would never have been possible in this country, if Englishmen had not become gradually accustomed, through the educational influences of the gross state of the laws of which I have just spoken, to despise the claims of women as such, and to cease, both in theory and in practice, to grant them that equality of citizenship which the Constitu-

[1] There are many other instances in English law besides these mentioned above, wherein the inequality of justice, as regards the two sexes, is grossly apparent. I cannot here however dwell upon this wide and painful subject. The following detached extracts bearing on the subject are taken from a chapter of the work of an American writer on "The English Common Law:"—"In the eye of the law, female chastity is only valuable for the work it can do. The custody of children belongs to the father; the mother has no right of control. The father may dispose of them as he sees fit. If there be a legal separation, and no special order of the Court, the custody of the children (except the nutriment of infants) belongs legally to the father." *Except the nutriment of infants!* here is a hint from the good God himself. Should we not think that the first time these words were written down, and men were compelled to see the natural dependence of the child upon the mother—to detect the obvious laws of nurture, natural and spiritual—the right of a good mother to her child would have made itself clear? In reference to the inequality of the divorce laws, this writer says—"In the late debate in Parliament on the new Divorce Bill, when a member objected to the introduction of a clause equalizing the relief of divorce to both sexes, he asked, 'If this clause were adopted, I should like to know how many married men there would be in this House?' He was answered by shouts of laughter! Would these

tion originally bestowed upon them.   The outrage upon
Lucretia put an end to the regal government in Rome ;
that upon Virginia proved the destruction of the power
of the Decemvirs ; an offence against a woman was the
occasion of the bloody vespers of Palermo.   In England, at this day, the cry, not of one, but of thousands
of outraged women is ascending, and entering into the
ears of the God of justice and of vengeance !

men have laughed, think you, if they had been asked how many
pure wives could be found in their family circles ? and if *not*, would
it have been because they were capable of estimating the value of
womanly virtue ? *No !* for that man cannot estimate womanly
virtue who has never known the worth of manly purity.   It would
be the spectres of illegitimacy and social ruin staring them in the
face, which would turn their lips so white ! In France (says the
Westminster Review) fidelity on the part of a husband is considered
a sort of imbecility.   What is thought of it in England ? Does this
scene in Parliament, printed for all our girls to read, suggest any
higher view ?"   " The laughter of fools," Solomon says, " is like
the crackling of thorns under a pot ;" but that laughter in the
English House of Commons was more like what one might expect
to hear—mingled with wailings—on approaching the gates of hell.

CHAPTER VIII.

I COME now to treat of the brighter and more hopeful side of the picture, and of the means whereby redress of the wrong lately perpetrated is to be obtained. De Lolme, after dwelling on the privileges of a people who live under a just code of laws, speaks as follows : " But all these privileges of the people, considered in themselves, may be but feeble defences against the real strength of those who govern : all these provisions, all these reciprocal rights, necessarily·suppose that things remain in their legal and settled course." And he goes on to suppose a case in which rulers, suddenly throwing themselves, as it were, out of the Constitution, and no longer respecting the person of the subject, should force upon the nation the enactments of an arbitrary will. He asks, "What then would be the people's resource ?" He answers, "It would be resistance."

He observes that the question of the right of the people to resistance, in certain cases, has been established by the laws of England, which look upon it as the "ultimate and láwful resource against the violences of power."[1] He further adds: "It was resistance that gave birth to the Great Charter, that lasting foundation of English liberty; and the excesses of a power established by force were also restrained by force. It has been by this same resistance that at different times the people have procured the confirmation of the same charter." Lastly, this resource of resistance, which for some time continued to be an act of force opposed to other acts of force was, at the era of our glorious Revolution, expressly recognised by the law itself.

Judge Blackstone, in his chapter on "the rights of persons," after examining the absolute rights which pertain to every Englishman, says, "But in vain would these rights be declared, ascertained, and protected by the dead letter of the law, if the Constitution had provided no other method to secure their actual enjoyment. It has therefore established certain other auxiliary rights of the subject, which serve principally as outworks or barriers to protect and maintain inviolate the three great and primary rights of personal security, personal liberty, and private property. . . .

" To vindicate these rights when actually violated or attacked, the subjects of England are entitled, in the

[1] De Lolme on the Constitution, p. 314.

K

first place, to the regular administration and free course
of justice in the courts of law.

" Next, to the right of petitioning the King and Parliament for redress of grievances.

" And lastly, to the right of having and using arms
for self-preservation and defence.

" And all these rights and liberties it is our birthright to enjoy entire."[1]

Now this solemn right of resistance, carrying with it,
as it does, great responsibilities, would be in itself but
a vain shadow, did there not exist in the nation the
means of effecting a general union, of bringing about
great and widely-spread co-operation, and, to use a
French word, that *solidarité* which are the requisite
conditions of success in any national enterprise for the
redress of national wrongs. Private individuals—and
most particularly is it the case in the instance of which
we are treating in this Essay—are forced to bear in silence
injuries in which they do not see other people take a
concern. They tremble in their solitude and weakness
at the formidable power of those who oppress them, and
as the latter well know the advantages of their own
position, they think they may venture upon anything.
But when, with the suffering of one—even the meanest
member—the sympathy of all the other members of

---

[1] Blackstone, Book i. p. 140 : " Rights of Persons."

the body politic comes to be expressed, and finds an organized utterance, then the throes of this agony begin at last to be felt as a simultaneous resistance to the power that inflicted it.

Lest there should be lurking in the minds of any of my readers the thought that Parliament is an authority which it is in vain to try to resist, and that we are to endure now from Parliament invasions of our rights more tyrannical than we should have endured formerly from a King, and therefore that we ought to sit still in inaction, or in a pusillanimous indifference and criminal submission to such invasions of our rights, I venture to urge the people of this country, by the noble examples of the past, to let no day pass over their head without some effort to effect the purification of our country from the great evil established in it by Parliament. And I cannot resist quoting here once more the words of that venerable peer, who has set us an example, worthy to be studied at this day, in resisting the encroachments of the Legislature. These words were spoken under the pressure of ill-health, and have in them a solemn pathos, to which the present crisis enables those of us who recognise its gravity to respond :—

" The constitution of this country has been openly invaded, in fact, and I have heard with horror and

astonishment, that very invasion defended upon principle. . . . My Lords, I thought the slavish doctrine of
passive obedience had long since been exploded. . . .
No man respects the House of Commons more than I
do, or would contend more strenuously than I would to
preserve them their just and legal authority. Within
the bounds prescribed by the constitution, that authority
is necessary to the well-being of the people; beyond
that line every exertion of power is arbitrary, is illegal,
it threatens tyranny to the people and destruction to the
State. Power without right is the most odious object
that can be offered to the human imagination. It is
not only pernicious to those who are subject to it, but
tends to its own destruction. . . . Tyranny, my Lords,
is detestable in every shape, but in none so formidable
as when it is assumed and exercised by a number of
tyrants. . . .

"My uncertain state of health must plead my excuse
if I wander from my argument; yet I thank God, my
Lords, for having thus long preserved so inconsiderable
a being as I am to take a part upon this great occasion,
and to contribute my endeavours, such as they are, to
restore, to save the constitution. My Lords, I need not
look abroad for grievances. The grand capital mischief
is fixed at home. It is corrupting the very foundation
of our political existence, and preying upon the vitals

of the State. The constitution has been grossly violated. THE CONSTITUTION AT THIS MOMENT STANDS VIOLATED. Until that wound be healed, until the grievance be redressed, it is in vain to recommend union to Parliament, in vain to promote concord among the people. If we mean seriously to unite the nation within itself, we must convince them that their complaints are regarded, that their injuries shall be redressed. On *that* foundation I would take the lead in recommending peace and harmony to the people. On any other I would never wish to see them united again. If the breach in the constitution be effectually repaired, the people will of themselves return to a state of tranquillity; if not, MAY DISCORD PREVAIL FOR EVER! If the king's servants will not permit the constitutional question to be decided according to the forms and on the principles of the constitution, it must then be decided in some other manner; and rather than it should be given up, rather than the nation should surrender their birthright to a despotic minister, I hope, my Lords, old as I am, I shall see the question brought to issue, and fairly tried between the people and the Government."[1]

Such words as these, however, indicate the struggles of a people whose representative government is so defective as not to offer a real representation, and who

[1] Lord Chatham's Speech on the case of Mr. Wilkes.

therefore are under the necessity, when their rulers do not represent them, of contemplating a violent resistance to their authority. We, on the contrary, now more happily situated, can contemplate a change by the ordinary course of elections of the individuals who represent us. The due action of this system under which we now live is well expressed in the words of De Lolme:—" When the rulers see that all their actions are exposed to public view, that in consequence of the celerity with which all things become communicated the whole nation forms, as it were, one continued *irritable body*, no part of which can be touched without exciting an universal *tremor*, they become sensible that the cause of each individual is really the cause of all, and that to attack the lowest among the people is to attack the whole people." [1]

Now it becomes of the greatest importance, seeing that the people are possessed of the power of awing the Legislature, that they should use it in the wisest and best manner ; and in order to that end we must bear in mind what has been so often proved to the glory of the people of England, that power is often most effectually expressed by an attitude of suspended determination. " Forming thus,[2] as it were, one body, the people at every instant have it in their power to strike the de-

---

[1] De Lolme, page 318.   [2] Page 321.

cisive blow which is to level everything. Like those
mechanical powers the greatest efficiency of which exists
at the instant which precedes their entering into action,
it has an immense force just because it does not yet
exert any, and in this state of stillness, but of suspense,
consists its true momentum."

Now it is this instant which precedes any direct
forcible action on the part of the people, which is the
instant most favourable for the conversion and enlightenment of those rulers who trespass upon the Constitution·
It is precisely at this instant that those who by virtue
of their commission from the people are intrusted with
the solemn responsibility of the more active part of
government, behold themselves, as it were, exposed to
public view, and attentively observed by men, not
fiercely, but solemnly and religiously bent on the recovery of their sacred rights; by men free from all
party spirit, and combined as men combine in a crisis
of common danger, and who place in their rulers only a
conditional trust. These rulers, feeling themselves thus
observed, are afraid of exciting commotion, revolution,
or rebellion, which, whatever else it effected, would
surely and certainly effect the destruction of their own
power, and be the close of their own tenure of office.
Under these circumstances, if they should have sacrificed
public liberties or been false to their trust, " they would

no sooner lift up their eyes towards that vast assembly which views them with this watchful attention, than they would find their public virtue return upon them, and would make haste to resume that plan of conduct out of the limits of which they can expect nothing but ruin and perdition." [1]

Therefore I trust you will pardon me, O patient and resolute people of England, who have in former national dangers so nobly borne, so long forborne, and so firmly acted, if I adjure you in the present crisis to remember the spirit in which your ancestors fought the battles of freedom, and to hold yourselves thoroughly prepared to *resist this legislation to the uttermost*, while cherishing the spirit of dependence on Divine aid, enjoined on the Hebrews of old in the words, "Stand still, and see the salvation of God." Remember that the great success attending your former acts of resistance, success which has been dwelt upon in wonder and admiration by our continental neighbours, is mainly owing to the fact that you influence rather than interfere, that you are able and prepared to strike, but refrain from striking.

"The power of the people is not when they strike, but when they keep their rulers in awe. It is when they can overthrow everything that they never need to move."

[1] De Lolme, page 322.

I have said that we live under a system of just laws,
and I have praised our representative government.
But we owe the existence of the Acts of Parliament
which we condemn, in a great measure to a grave fault
in these laws, and a grave inadequacy in that representative government. I have already spoken of that
fault in our laws. It cannot be expected that due attention will ever be paid to the interests of any class
which is not duly represented in the government of the
country. If women had possessed the franchise, the
Contagious Diseases Acts could not have been passed.
I have preferred in this Essay to treat these Acts as a
matter affecting the whole community rather than as
one which concerns women particularly, inasmuch as
the claims which women and men have to jury trial
and to all constitutional rights are equal, and rest
on the same foundation, which cannot be destroyed for
one sex only. I can never view this question as fundamentally any more a woman's question than it is a
man's. These Acts secure the enslavement of women
and the increased immorality of men; and history and
experience alike teach us that these two results are
never separated. Slavery and immorality lead to de-
gradation, political ruin, and intellectual decay, and
therefore it is that these Acts are a question for the
whole nation at large. Yet we cannot shut our eyes

to the fact that these Acts of Parliament in the first
instance affect women only; it is by their necessary
consequences, not by their immediate action, that men
also are affected.

It is the beneficent arrangement of God that the
interests of men and of women are identical; to this
we owe it that women have not been more the sufferers
from the partial representative system of this country
than they have yet been. But let us not forget that
the same great ordinance of God holds equally of the
interests of all mankind, in all lands, and of all ranks;
the interests of all are identical; yet there are oppressions manifold among mankind. It is to the recognition which necessarily follows sooner or later of that
great law of God, that we may, under Providence, attribute the fact that the world is not worse than it is. For
when men act in neglect of this great law, evils ensue
more or less immediately; if they continue so to act,
their neglect of this law brings eventually disturbance
or decay, and an overturning of the fabric of society.

The object of a complete representation of the people
is to establish a government which, by its own natural
action, shall follow out and not violate this great principle. Hence it is that a just representative government—that is, one in which there is no class unre-
presented—is the only form of government which bears

in itself the elements and means of its own continuance
or revival. All other governments bear in them the
necessary seeds of revolution; they must all be cor-
rected from without; it alone is able to correct itself
from within. The possession of the franchise by women
is not only the pledge of security for women—the only
satisfactory pledge that the interests of women shall be
duly respected,—but it is also the pledge of security for
the nation that it shall not be in danger of violating
the great principle, that the interests of all are identical,
and shall not therefore incur the evil consequences of
such a violation.

The object of representative government is to make
the recognition of the principle that the interests of all
are identical, preventive rather than remedial. What
I mean by this will be best illustrated by the very case
with which we are dealing. The Contagious Diseases
Acts are based on the fundamental assumption that
the interests of women, as a class, can be neglected,
while those of men can be cherished. It is an
erroneous basis on which to make any law, for it is a
contradiction of the law of God. Evil fruits must
always follow for the whole nation which permits
its rulers to act on such an assumption. In the case
in point these evil fruits are easily detected, and the
fatal operation of the bad principle is easily traced;

hence those who already possess the franchise may be trusted to repeal these Acts. But though in this instance the path of return from error may be short, still it is a path of *return*. It is a retracing of our steps, the necessity of which has been brought about by abnormal conditions; and there exists in our representative government no guarantee against the repetition of such errors in the future. The nation has to be recalled from error to rectitude; it has to purge itself; to recover a great principle; and if God grant that it returns to that principle from the expectation rather than from the experience of the miseries of violating it, that result will be one which does not flow naturally from our present partial representative system, but which has been induced upon it from without. The aim of representative government is to make the recognition of the identity of the interests of all a continual and natural process; and until women have votes, that which stands between this nation and the evil consequences of violating this principle is only the precarious barrier of "agitation." Until women possess the franchise the system of our government will be unstable and not self-corrective. And this is much more evident in the present day than in former times, and is daily becoming more evident. There are great social questions pressing for consideration and for settlement; and so long as one sex undertakes to consider these questions alone, we shall be hurried into errors similar to the Contagious Diseases Acts, and into legislation based upon the neglect of the interests of women—a neglect which in all instances will prove, as in this it most emphatically proves, fatal to those imagined interests on behalf of which these are neglected. Legislation can never in these days, and at the stage of civilisation which we have reached, be just and pure until women are represented. Do not let the reader here for a moment suppose that I am attributing to men any intentional injustice, or that I am supposing that they will be actuated in general by anything but benevolent intentions towards women. But the safety and stability of all that is done in the nation depends, not upon the benevolent intentions of the enfranchised towards the unenfranchised, but upon the just representation of all. Self-government is life, and life cannot be lived at second-hand.

"Unfinished questions have no pity for the repose of nations." It is only by means of the joint action of men and women that the great social questions of the present day can ever be satisfactorily settled, and when the iniquitous Contagious Diseases Acts—that huge retrograde step in legislation—are done away with, the country will only fall into new errors unless the voice of the women of the country, now raised from without, receive that permanent means of expressing itself shortly, easily, and effectually, which is given by the possession of the franchise, and by that alone. Let it not be forgotten that the women of England have had to come forth from the retirement of their own loved homes, to do and to suffer what they never would have been required to do and to suffer if they had possessed the franchise, and to wear their lives out in protesting against an iniquity which—if their unenfranchised voices be not powerful enough—will prove the ruin of their country. Those fastidious gentlemen who querulously cry out against the attitude lately assumed by patriotic and Christian women, and who shudder lest the faintest echoes of this agitation should reach the refined ears of their own wives and daughters, should remember that agitations involving questions of deep domestic interest will again and again be necessary, unless women are granted the power to influence Parliament without such agitation. It would be well that such persons should be fully alive to the fact also, that English women will be found ready again and again to agitate, to give men no repose, to turn the world upside down if need be, until impurity and injustice are expelled from our laws. The interests of women are palpably identical with morality; that the interests of

men are equally so is not yet clearly perceived by
all men.   While contending for justice to their sex,
women will therefore contend for morality.   Let those
who consider it an evil that feminine voices should be
heard, even in the cause of morality, in such an agitation as the present, endeavour to prevent a recurrence
of the evil by putting it in the power of women to act
for the good of the country without raising their voice
aloud.

CHAPTER IX.

I HAVE now shown the grave character of the question which we are discussing. I have stated the principles of Magna Charta which form the basis of our Constitution, and I have pointed out how these principles are violated by the Acts which we oppose; I have traced the pernicious consequences arising from this violation, politically as well as morally; and I have briefly indicated the means by which we may repair the breach which has been made.

A question which involves not only the principles of morality but the fundamental principles of our liberties, must be referred for its final decision to no meaner tribunal than that of the entire people. That people is the only tribunal competent to decide a question so vital as this, which affects every individual in the nation, and must colour the whole of the future internal policy of England. In retaining or rejecting these Acts we have now to determine whether our Constitution shall stand as it has stood hitherto, or whether it

shall be changed. This question can only be determined by that power in whose hands the Constitution is ultimately vested. The determination of this
momentous question will involve also the fate of all that
legislation the tendency of which, during the last century,
has been gradually to weaken the Constitution through
the insidious rejection in a large number of cases of that
great safeguard of our liberties, Jury Trial. Had not the
way been paved for such arbitrary Acts as those which
we oppose, by the innovations which our great constitutional lawyers have so deplored, it would have been
impossible for Parliament to have escaped arousing the
alarm of the people when it proposed this present
wholesale breach of the great principles of English jurisprudence. But the present Acts have opened our eyes
to the nature and tendency of those encroachments
which have long been silently going on among us, and
we now see it to be a strong argument against such
encroachments that they should have culminated in
such an invasion of our rights. Men will carelessly
tolerate for a long time encroachments in cases of little
moment, if these encroachments tend towards the ease
and expedition of justice; but when they find that
under colour of that ease or expedition, men prompted
by selfishness and fear, have made a law which hands
over a vast multitude of the people into the power of

L

the lowest of the executive, the real worth of our country begins to appear, and rather than tolerate such an evil they will abolish that whole system, so far as it relates to criminal cases, if that system can successfully be pleaded as an excuse for such treachery on the part of our rulers.[1]

What tribunal then can decide so grave and important a national question as this, other than the nation itself? What therefore shall we think of a Government which, when the nation has pressed this question upon it, has shown itself so contemptuous of the great constitutional principle involved, as to profess to investigate the question by means of a tribunal of twenty-six men, a considerable proportion of whom rank among the actual framers or supporters of the Acts? Further, in what light must it appear to us when we learn that the investigation conducted by this tribunal is expressly to be made into the " operation and administration " of the Acts, and that it has no other specified object? Those who made such a limitation must surely either have been ignorant

[1] " I think with you that the extension and multiplication of such proceedings and Acts of Parliament is a grave constitutional peril, as I have said elsewhere. I think it of the greatest importance that the constitutional iniquity implied in the Contagious Diseases Acts should be fully exposed to the eyes of the whole country. It is one of the dangers of popular government that the people lose their proper suspicion of the executive and their reverence for constitutional bulwarks."—Letter from Sheldon Amos, Esq., Professor of Jurisprudence.

of, or determined to override, the constitutional objections which the nation itself has proclaimed more or less distinctly from the first; otherwise why was not the inquiry directed at least in part to that momentous question on which it must finally be decided?

A Royal Commission has been appointed to inquire into these Acts.   What is the subject of their inquiry? Is it whether this law be consistent with the first principles of morality?   No, for that, such a tribunal, not being the ultimate fount of truth, is incompetent; nor, since we have each of us direct access to the ultimate fount of truth, do we need its verdict on this point. Is it whether this law be consistent or not with the principles of the English Constitution?   No, although into this question inquiry might well have been made by such a body, for there are constitutional lawyers amongst us who could not on inquiry have remained blind to the fact of this great violation of our rights. But such an inquiry apparently did not suit the Government; therefore, what do they inquire into? Merely into this question, How does this double violation of the constitution and of morality work?

Whatever, therefore, be the verdict of this Commission, it obviously cannot affect either of these vital questions, which must be tried by the whole nation; and the decision of this Commission, worthless if it be for extension, is equally worthless if it be for repeal, because these Acts, if repealed on that verdict, would then be repealed on the ground of their unsatisfactory operation. The evil principle would not only be left undisputed and unrebuked, but it would be practically admitted that our constitutional privileges may again be violated should the results of such violation be temporarily satisfactory. Therefore I unhesitatingly venture to assert, that if the verdict of this Royal Commission should be for repeal, it would be more hurtful to our national interests than if it should report for extension, because, as it must be evident, the Acts would then be repealed on the ground of their medical inoperativeness, or the difficulty of their administration, or for some reason short of their constitutional iniquity, and not—as they will be when repealed by the people— on the ground and by reason of their essential wickedness as violations of morality and constitutional liberty. Surely it was the guardian genius of our Constitution who so happily blinded the Government which passed this law, as to permit it to assign and limit the grounds of this inquiry, as it has done, and has thus led it to throw upon the people themselves the necessity and duty, not only of repealing these Acts, but of forcing Parliament to place on the Statute-book a lasting record of this bitter conflict, in the form of a Statute which shall bind our Legislature for all future ages to regard as sacred the constitutional rights of the people, and which shall make it impossible for it again thus to violate the Constitution.

The great restraining Statutes which exist in England have grown out of aggressions made by those in power; and were not some unusual aggressions periodically to call for the renewal of such restraints, our Constitution might slip out of our hands without our being aware of it. Such restraints as these are as necessary now as they were in ancient times; nor will the progress of civilisation or the diffusion of education ever preclude the necessity of such ever-renewed restraints. For no diffusion of the ideas of liberty, no universal admission and universal acceptance of the doctrine of personal freedom, no acuteness of perception of the necessity of political equality for the very existence of a State, can ever eradicate from the hearts of men those passions and instincts which have been, in all ages and in all countries, the cause of the destruction of liberty. For liberties are not undermined for the sake of undermining liberties. The Constitution is not attacked with the motive of destroying it; but in all ages and in all countries liberties have been undermined, and constitutions have been invaded, not for those ends directly, but for the immediate end of some private passion or some private lust which is inconsistent with public liberty, and which can only be gained by its overthrow.

Let me therefore press upon my readers to remember that when we have obtained the repeal of these obnoxious Statutes, our work is then only half done. Besides that negative action, a positive action is called for, and means have to be taken to prevent the recurrence of such an invasion and such a struggle. Unless this be done, we are not safe for more than a generation. When we who have fought this battle are laid in our graves, when at some future time those who succeed us may be less vigilant or more enduring than we, and when at the same time men in power may be actuated by the same ever-recurring instincts of passion and self-interest—instincts which are always at the root of the destruction of freedom,—then our liberties may be irretrievably lost, and we shall be to blame for it, unless we have at the present crisis, as our forefathers have done, placed on the records of Parliament a solemn and binding agreement between the people and its rulers, whereby each shall be strictly bound to conform to their respective obligations.

Guizot remarks, in speaking of the success of English revolutions :—" It is not enough that rights should be recognised and promises made, it is further necessary that these rights should be respected, and these promises fulfilled; the last article therefore of the Great Charter is especially intended to provide this guarantee. It is there said that the barons shall elect twenty-five by their own free choice, charged to exercise all vigilance that the provisions of the charter may never fail to be carried into effect. The powers of these twenty-five barons (a kind of vigilance committee) were unlimited." If the king or his agents allowed themselves to violate the enactments of the charter in the very smallest particular, the barons were to denounce this abuse before the king, and demand that it should be instantly checked. If the king did not accede to their demand, the barons had the right, forty days after the summons had been issued by them, to prosecute the king, to deprive him of all his lands and castles, " the safety of his person, the queen and his children being respected," until the abuse had been reformed to the satisfaction of the barons and of the whole nation.[1]

[1] I may just quote further the solemn words to which the king was compelled to give his signature, which are contained in this guaranteeing clause of Magna Charta : " Whereas for the honour of God and the amendment of our kingdom, and for the better quieting the discord that has arisen between us and our barons, we have granted all these things aforesaid ; being willing to render them firm and lasting, we do give and grant our subjects the under-written security, namely, that the barons may choose five-and-twenty barons whom they think convenient, who shall take care with all their might to hold and observe, and cause to be observed,

Any one who reads the History of England may judge for himself of the wisdom of these immortal restraining Statutes called the Petition of Rights and Bill of Rights, which were made necessary by the aggressions and illegal actions of subsequent monarchs. And in less terrible crises than those which called for these great confirmatory charters, it has been invariably the habit of the English people to claim, through Parliament, besides the redress of the wrong committed, some similar wholesome restraining Statute, elucidating and strengthening anew that particular part of the Constitution which may happen to have been imperilled, and securing that similar violations shall not, in future, be attempted with impunity. Among these may be reckoned the famous Habeas Corpus Act, and a multitude of others which it is needless here to recount.

It would be improper for me to conclude this Essay, in which I have pointed out the similarity of the present crises to others in past history, without calling the reader's attention to one characteristic in which these

the peace and liberties we have granted them, and by this our present Charter confirmed ; so that if we, our justiciary, our bailiffs, or any of our officers, shall in any circumstance fail in the performance of them towards any person, or shall break through any of these articles of peace and security, the said barons shall"—and here follows the account of the prosecution to which the king agrees to submit himself.

Acts of Parliament stand pre-eminent in the history of our legislation. The tyrannical aggressions of those in power. in former days were indeed always the fruit of lust in some form or other,—greed of gain, or personal influence,. personal pleasure, jealousy, or revenge; yet the effect of those aggressions was not so directly as in the present case to make the people immoral. The immorality was at first. at least confined to the aggressor. He assailed the liberties only of the subject, and in so doing struck, no doubt, more or less remotely, at the root of public virtue; but he did not proclaim a vicious moral code in the ears of the whole people. Now this last tyrannous aggression has sown broadcast the seeds of an immoral principle. This is a law which not only proceeds of evil, but immediately results in evil, by forcing a moral iniquity upon the people. It is pre-eminently an onslaught on morality, while it is an attack on the Constitution. Therefore in order to oppose this great twofold evil, we need, not only the revival of all our English patriotism, our love of freedom and of justice, but a deeper revival still, that of the soul and of the spirit. We need a renewal of faith in divine and eternal principles, a moral regeneration, a practical return to the simplicity of Christ.

Guizot, in speaking of the secret of the success of the English Revolution, says that in spite of the moral

scepticism of the times " the mass of the people remained faithful to simple Christianity,—as much
attached to their doctrines as to their liberties. The
views of the citizen, of the freeholder, and even of the
peasant, soared far above his actual condition. He was
a Christian ; in his family or among his friends he
boldly studied the mysteries of Divine power ; what
earthly power, he asked, could be so high that he must
abstain from considering it ? In the Sacred Scriptures
he read the laws of God ; to render obedience to them
he was forced to resist other laws ; it therefore became
necessary to him to ascertain where human legislation
ought to terminate." It is this alternative which, in a
much more marked and naked form than ever before,
our citizens, our freeholders, and our peasants are once
more driven to contemplate face to face ; and the question, " Shall we obey God or man ?" is that which they
are now called upon once more to answer.

The whole conduct of the resistance in which we are
now engaged to this immoral and arbitrary law will depend
upon the sincerity and depth of the religious principle
of this country. A moral and spiritual conviction must
be the heart and soul of our present movement.
Already it is proved to be so, and will be more fully
proved ere the struggle be ended. Already that revival
of moral faith, the simultaneousness of which with the

rapid advances of a materialistic creed rests upon the promise of God himself, is beginning to prove its force as the most potent agency for political reform. Already it is gathering into a compact company the grave, the virtuous, the religious throughout the land.

It would be unseasonable at the close of this Essay for me to approach that difficult question which must needs, at times, trouble the minds of thoughtful persons who try to read the tendencies of the age; I mean the subtle connection between democracy and despotism— the tendency of democratic nations to combine the idea of a strongly centralized, ubiquitous, and omnipotent government with that of the sovereignty of the people, a combination which, when fully realized, makes every man willing to put himself in leading-strings, because it is not a person, nor a class of persons, but the people at large that holds the end of his chain; but before closing these remarks I venture to address a word of caution to my readers among the working classes who are electors. There are persons of birth, of station, spoiled, it may be, by the long inheritance of privilege, who hate the Constitution because of the barriers which it places between themselves and the accomplishment from time to time of certain arbitrary designs, and because in general, in a noble degree, it is no " respecter of persons." On the other hand, there are men—and among them are some who loudly profess to be the people's friends—who *despise* the Constitution, and who see without a regret the invasion of its fundamental principles,—principles which they affect to believe are obsolete. When, therefore, the time comes, once and again, for you to look around you to select men to represent you in Parliament, and when gentlemen come forward professing the Radical principles which the majority of you uphold, pause for a moment! for among these professors there are some such as those to whom I allude, who despise the Constitution. Myself a Liberal, and an admirer of republican[1] institutions, I venture to advise you to regard this class of political aspirants with extreme suspicion. Withhold from them your confidence until you have thoroughly sounded their principles. Those to whom I allude are for the most part young men, or men at least characterized by that immaturity of judgment which is not the exclusive attribute of youth. They talk loudly of a future Republic, while they are at heart, though it may be unconsciously so, the prophets and devotees of the despotism of the future—that despotism which may consist with democratical institutions, and which may prove to be the most terrible of all tyrannies. You will

---

[1] Whether as they may exist under a limited monarchy, or, as in America, under a President.

scarcely fail to detect this tendency in the conversation
of these men, who sometimes possess more of University
cultivation than knowledge of the Constitution of England or experience of life. You will hear them speak
with approbation of the most sweeping and compulsory
measures ; you will find them betraying a contempt for
individual freedom, and a readiness to sacrifice the
rights of persons, however sacred, to the interests of the
" sovereign people," represented by an arbitrary, centralized, imperial government. Sheltered under the
idea of the sovereignty of the people, they find it possible
to foster many a project destructive of individual freedom. It is to be feared that when such persons come
into positions of power they will carry out these tendencies into practice. Adopting all the institutions
of a democratical community as their basis, thereby
appealing to your sympathy and winning your confidence, they will (not wilfully perhaps, but through a
natural love of domination, or from mere thoughtlessness
and immaturity of mind)[1] contribute to reduce their

<hr/>

[1] The celebrated Count Oxenstiern, Chancellor of Sweden, one
day when his son was expressing to him his diffidence of his own
abilities, and the dread with which he thought of ever engaging in
the management of public affairs, made the following Latin answer
to him : " Nescis, mi fili, quantulâ sapientia regitur mundus"
—" You know not, my son, with what little wisdom the world is
governed."
A young Member of Parliament, recently elected, remarked to me

republic of the future to that state of society described
by De Tocqueville—a man who fully acquiesced in and
sympathized with the republican development of his
day, but saw its dangers. " The supreme power in such
a democracy," he says, " extends its arm over the whole
community ; it covers the surface of society with a net-
work of small complicated rules, minute and uniform,
through which the most original minds and most energetic characters cannot penetrate to rise above the
crowd. The will of man is not shattered, but softened
and made weak ; such a power does not destroy, but it
prevents existence ; it does not tyrannize, but it com-
presses, enervates, extinguishes, and stupifies a people ;
. . . it every day renders the exercise of the free agency
of man less useful and less frequent ; it circumscribes
the will within a narrower range, and gradually robs a
man of all the uses of himself.—I think," he says
elsewhere, " that the species of oppression by which
democratic nations are menaced is unlike anything
which before existed in the world : our contemporaries
will find no prototype of it in their memories. . . .
I have been led to think that the nations of Christen-
dom will perhaps eventually undergo some sort of

one day : " When one gets into Parliament, one sees that a great
nation is after all like an old goat whom anybody may lead by the
beard ! "

oppression like that which hung over several of the nations of the ancient world."[1] A Greek sage observed long ago that the strongest oligarchies are those which in themselves were democratical. The possibility of such a future despotism need not however be regarded with dread by a people long trained to freedom, and watchful for the interests of all. I believe that we may escape subjection to this despotism of the future, which is shadowed forth in the crude and anomalous theories of the politicians to whom I have alluded, by holding fast those very principles by the strength of which our people have been enabled so happily in times past to resist monarchical aggressions. The vital source for the nourishment of those principles is a deep conviction of the Divine government of the world, and of the worth of every soul created by God. " If," says De Tocqueville, "amongst the opinions of a democratic people any of those pernicious theories exist which inculcate that all perishes with the body, let the men by whom such theories are professed be marked as the natural foes of such a people. The Materialists are offensive to me in many respects; I am disgusted at their arrogance. If their system could be of any utility to man, it would seem to be by giving him a modest opinion of himself. But these reasoners show that it is not so; and when

[1] *Democracy in America,* vol. iii. chap. 6.

they think they have said enough to establish that they
are brutes, they show themselves as proud as if they
had demonstrated that they are gods."[1]   We have
lately seen this arrogant materialism culminate in a
temper of mind well expressed by one of the writers in
the organ of the fashionable London Clubs, where,
treating of that large class of persons of various shades
of character who are brought under the Contagious
Diseases Acts, he says these women ought to be
" treated as foul sewers are treated, as physical facts
and not as moral agents."   Sewers have neither souls
nor civil rights ; by admitting into their political theory
the idea that any class of human beings whatever may
be reduced to the level of an inanimate nuisance for
political purposes, these writers have demonstrated to
us very clearly the intimate connection between a gross
materialism and the most cruel and oppressive despotism.   The men who speak thus, and who act in
harmony with their utterances, do not believe that the
beings of whom they speak have souls ; to them any
regenerating influence from a Divine source upon the
spirit of man or woman is inconceivable.   It is needless
to indicate more particularly the natural and close
alliance between this materialism and the coercive and
oppressive policy which such materialists, though fre-

---

[1] *Democracy in America*, vol. iii. p. 297.

quently professing radicalism, will readily adopt, merely transferring the power of the deprivation of civil and human rights from the hands of a monarch or a hereditary aristocracy into those of official experts who will be the elect of a fully enfranchised people, and therefore more dangerously confided in by the people. In order that we may avoid such a future despotism having its root deeply laid in a materialistic creed, we need—and a merciful God will grant it—for each individual, and for the nation at large, a fuller measure of that light of the conscience, and that life of the spirit which will enable us to discern with clearness and to tread with perseverance that path which leads to the goal whither the hopes of the human race are ever tending.

The following are the editions of some books consulted :—

De Tocqueville's Democracy in America. Third edition. Saunders and Otley.

Blackstone's Commentaries. Thirteenth edition, with Christian's Notes.

De Lolme on the Constitution. Second edition. Wilkie and Robinson.

Creasy on the Constitution. Eighth edition. Bentley.

Guizot's Causes of the Success of the English Revolution. Murray.

APPENDIX A.

DE TOCQUEVILLE says on Jury Trial, "To look upon the jury as a mere judicial institution, is to confine our attention to a very narrow view of it; for however great its influence may be upon the decisions of the law courts, that influence is very subordinate to the powerful effects which it produces on the destinies of the community at large. The jury is above all a political institution, and it must be regarded in this light to be fully appreciated.

" The institution of the jury may be aristocratic or democratic, according to the class of society from which the jurors are selected ; but it always preserves its republican character, inasmuch as it places the real direction of society in the hands of the governed, or of a portion of the governed, instead of leaving it under the authority of the Government. . . . . The true sanction of political laws is to be found in penal legislation, and if that sanction be wanting, the law will sooner or later lose its cogency. He who punishes infractions of the law is the real master of society. Now, the institution of the jury raises the people itself, or at least a class of citizens, to the bench of judicial authority. The institution of the jury consequently invests the people, or that class of citizens, with the direction of society.
. . . . The jury serves to communicate the spirit of the

judges to the minds of the citizens; and this spirit, with the habits which attend it, is the soundest preparation for free institutions." [1]   Thus, while in England we are gradually allowing the institution of the jury to fall into disuse, we are making the central executive the real master of society, and while we imagine we are advancing towards a more strongly republican character, we are in fact retrograding towards imperialism.

APPENDIX B.

In the Act passed 6th August 1861, "To consolidate and amend the statute law of England and Ireland relating to larceny and other similar offences," 24 and 25 Victoria, chapter 96, there is, by clause 110, an appeal allowed in summary cases as follows :—

24 and 25 Vict. ch. 96, s. 110—" In all cases where the sum adjudged to be paid on any summary conviction shall exceed five pounds, or the imprisonment adjudged shall exceed one month, or the conviction shall take place before one justice only, any person who shall think himself aggrieved by any such conviction may appeal to the next Court of General or Quarter Sessions, which shall be holden not less than twelve days after the day of such conviction, for the county or place wherein the cause of complaint shall have arisen; provided that such person shall give to the complainant a notice in writing of such appeal, and of the cause and matter thereof, within three days after such conviction, and seven clear days at the least before such

---

[1] *Democracy in America*, vol. ii. p. 115.

Sessions, and shall also either remain in custody until the Sessions, or shall enter into a recognizance with two sufficient sureties," etc. etc.

This appeal clause is identical with that in 24 and 25 Vict. c. 97, and continually repeated in other Acts of Parliament, as, for instance, in the one against brawling in church, etc. etc. It will be seen therefore that the absence of a right to appeal from the conviction by the justice of the peace under the Contagious Diseases Acts is a peculiar harshness of these Acts, as contrasted with general criminal Acts.

It appears from the "Criminal Law Amendment Acts," 24 and 25 Vict. c. 96, 97, and 100, that the largest fine that can be inflicted by a justice of the peace is £50, which large fine can apparently be inflicted only in one case, viz., that of wounding deer (see c. 96, s. 12). Generally the limiting fine is £20 or £5. The greatest punishment mentioned in these Acts, as assignable by a justice of the peace, is *six months' imprisonment*. Now, under the Contagious Diseases Acts (clause 7, Act 1869) the woman can be imprisoned in hospital for *nine months*. (By clause 24, Act 1866, the period during which she could be thus imprisoned was limited to six months, but was extended to nine months by clause 7, Act 1869. This extension, in common with many other features, shows the insidious character of these Acts.)

In addition, therefore, to the fundamental and absolute points of difference mentioned in the text of this Essay, these Acts differ from all previous Criminal Acts—1st, In inflicting a longer imprisonment on summary conviction; and 2d, In not permitting the appeal allowed under other Criminal Acts.

EDINBURGH : PRINTED BY THOMAS AND ARCHIBALD CONSTABLE,
PRINTERS TO THE QUEEN, AND TO THE UNIVERSITY.

88 PRINCES STREET,
Edinburgh, Feb. 1st, 1871.

EDMONSTON & DOUGLAS'
LIST OF WORKS

———oOo———

The Culture and Discipline of the Mind, and other Essays.
By JOHN ABERCROMBIE, M.D. New Edition. Fcap. 8vo, cloth, 3s. 6d.

Wanderings of a Naturalist in India,
The Western Himalayas, and Cashmere. By DR. A. L. ADAMS of the 22d Regiment. 8vo, with Illustrations, price 10s. 6d.
"The author need be under no apprehension of wearying his readers. . . He prominently combines the sportsman with the naturalist."—*Sporting Review.*

Notes of a Naturalist in the Nile Valley and Malta.
By ANDREW LEITH ADAMS. Author of "Wanderings of a Naturalist in India." Crown 8vo, with Illustrations, price 15s.
"Most attractively instructive to the general reader."—*Bell's Messenger.*

Alexandra Feodorowna, late Empress of Russia.
By A. TH. VON GRIMM, translated by LADY WALLACE. 2 vols. 8vo, with Portraits, price 21s.
"Contains an amount of information concerning Russian affairs and Russian society."—*Morning Post.*

Always in the Way.
By the author of 'The Tommiebeg Shootings.' 12mo, price 1s. 6d.

The Malformations, Diseases, and Injuries of the Fingers
and Toes, and their Surgical Treatment. By THOMAS ANNANDALE, F.R.C.S., 8vo, with Illustrations, price 10s. 6d.

Odal Rights and Feudal Wrongs.
A Memorial for Orkney. By DAVID BALFOUR of Balfour and Trenaby. 8vo, price 6s.

Sermons by the late James Bannerman, D.D., Professor of
Apologetics and Pastoral Theology, New College, Edinburgh. In 1 vol., extra fcap. 8vo, price 5s.

The Life, Character, and Writings of Benjamin Bell,
F.R.C.S.E., F.R.S.E. Author of a 'System of Surgery,' and other Works. By his Grandson, BENJAMIN BELL, F.R.C.S.E. Fcap. 8vo, price 3s. 6d.

The Holy Grail. An Inquiry into the Origin and Signifi-
cation of the Romances of the San Grëal. By Dr. F. G. BERGMANN. Fcap. 8vo, price 1s. 6d.

"Contains, in a short space, a carefully-expressed account of " the romances of chivalry, which compose what has been called the Epic cycle of the San Grëal."— *Athenæum.*

Homer and the Iliad.
In Three Parts. By JOHN STUART BLACKIE, Professor of Greek in the University of Edinburgh. 4 vols. demy 8vo, price 42s.

By the same Author.

On Democracy.
Sixth Edition, price 1s.

Musa Burschicosa.
A Book of Songs for Students and University Men. Fcap. 8vo, price 2s. 6d.

War Songs of the Germans, translated, with the Music, and
Historical Illustrations of the Liberation War and the Rhine Boundary Question. Fcap. 8vo, price 2s. 6d. cloth, 2s. paper. *Dedicated to Thomas Carlyle.*

On Greek Pronunciation.
Demy 8vo, 3s. 6d.

Political Tracts.
No. 1. GOVERNMENT. No. 2. EDUCATION. Price 1s. each.

On Beauty.   **Lyrical Poems.**
Crown 8vo, cloth, 8s. 6d.   Crown 8vo, cloth, 7s. 6d.

The New Picture Book.
Pictorial Lessons on Form, Comparison, and Number, for Children under Seven Years of Age. With Explanations by NICHOLAS BOHNY. **Fifth Edition.** 36 oblong folio coloured Illustrations. Price 7s. 6d.

The Home Life of Sir David Brewster.
By his daughter, Mrs. GORDON. 2d Edition. Crown 8vo, price 6s.

"With his own countrymen it is sure of a welcome, and to the *savants* of Europe, and of the New World, it will have a real and special interest of its own. —*Pall Mall Gazette.*

France under Richelieu and Colbert.
By J. H. BRIDGES, M.B. Small 8vo, price 8s. 6d.

Works by John Brown, M.D., F.R.S.E.
LOCKE AND SYDENHAM. Extra fcap. 8vo, price 7s. 6d.

HORÆ SUBSECIVÆ. Sixth Edition. Extra fcap. 8vo, price 7s. 6d.

LETTER TO THE REV. JOHN CAIRNS, D.D. Second Edition, crown 8vo, sewed, 2s.

ARTHUR H. HALLAM; Extracted from 'Horæ Subsecivæ.' Fcap. sewed, 2s. ; cloth, 2s. 6d.

RAB AND HIS FRIENDS; Extracted from 'Horæ Subsecivæ.' Forty-sixth thousand. Fcap. sewed, 6d.

MARJORIE FLEMING : A Sketch. Fifteenth thousand. Fcap. sewed, 6d.

OUR DOGS; Extracted from 'Horæ Subsecivæ.' Nineteenth thousand. Fcap. sewed, 6d.

RAB AND HIS FRIENDS. With Illustrations by Sir George Harvey, R.S.A., Sir J. Noel Paton, R.S.A., and J. B. New Edition, small quarto, cloth, price 3s. 6d.

"WITH BRAINS, SIR ;" Extracted from 'Horæ Subsecivæ.' Fcap. sewed, 6d.

MINCHMOOR. Fcap. sewed, 6d.

JEEMS THE DOORKEEPER : A Lay Sermon. Price 6d.

THE ENTERKIN. Price 6d.

Memoirs of John Brown, D.D.
By the Rev. J. CAIRNS, D.D., Berwick, with Supplementary Chapter by his Son, JOHN BROWN, M.D. Fcap. 8vo, cloth, 9s. 6d.

The Biography of Samson
Illustrated and Applied. By the REV. JOHN BRUCE, D.D., Minister of Free St. Andrew's Church, Edinburgh. Second Edition. 18mo, cloth, 2s.

The Life of Gideon.
By Rev. JOHN BRUCE, D.D., Free St. Andrew's Church, Edinburgh. 1 vol. fcap. 8vo, price 5s.

"We commend this able and admirable volume to the cordial acceptance of our readers.—*Daily Review.*

Tragic Dramas from History.
By ROBERT BUCHANAN, M.A., late Professor of Logic and Rhetoric in the University of Glasgow. 2 vols. fcap. 8vo, price 12s.

By the Loch and River Side.
Forty Graphic Illustrations by a New Hand. Oblong folio, handsomely bound, 21s.

The De Oratore of Cicero.
Translated by F. B. CALVERT, M.A. Crown 8vo, price 7s. 6d.

My Indian Journal,
Containing descriptions of the principal Field Sports of India, with Notes on the Natural History and Habits of the Wild Animals of the Country. By COLONEL WALTER CAMPBELL, author of 'The Old Forest Ranger.' 8vo, with Illustrations, price 16s.

Popular Tales of the West Highlands,
Orally Collected, with a translation by J. F. CAMPBELL. 4 vols. extra fcap. cloth, 32s.

Inaugural Address at Edinburgh,
April 2, 1866, by THOMAS CARLYLE, on being Installed as Rector of the University there. Price 1s.

On the Constitution of Papal Conclaves.

By W. C. CARTWRIGHT, M.P. Fcap. 8vo, price 6s. 6d.

A book which will, we believe, charm careful students of history, while it will dissipate much of the ignorance which in this country surrounds the subject. —*Spectator.*

Gustave Bergenroth. A Memorial Sketch.

By W. C. CARTWRIGHT, M.P. Author of "The Constitution of Papal Conclaves." Crown 8vo, price 7s. 6d.

"To those who knew this accomplished student, Mr. Cartwright's enthusiastic memoirs will be very welcome.—*Standard.*

Life and Works of Rev. Thomas Chalmers, D.D., LL.D.

MEMOIRS OF THE REV. THOMAS CHALMERS. By REV. W. HANNA, D.D., LL.D. 4 vols., 8vo, cloth, £2 : 2s.

—— Cheap Edition, 2 vols., crown 8vo, cloth, 12s.

POSTHUMOUS WORKS, 9 vols., 8vo—

Daily Scripture Readings, 3 vols., £1 : 11 : 6. Sabbath Scripture Readings, 2 vols., £1 : 1s. Sermons, 1 vol., 10s. 6d. Institutes of Theology, 2 vols., £1 : 1s. Prelections on Butler's Analogy, etc., 1 vol., 10s. 6d.

Sabbath Scripture Readings. Cheap Edition, 2 vols., crown 8vo, 10s.

Daily Scripture Readings. Cheap Edition, 2 vols., crown 8vo, 10s.

ASTRONOMICAL DISCOURSES, 1s. COMMERCIAL DISCOURSES, 1s.

SELECT WORKS, in 12 vols., crown 8vo, cloth, per vol., 6s.

Lectures on the Romans, 2 vols. Sermons, 2 vols. Natural Theology, Lectures on Butler's Analogy, etc., 1 vol. Christian Evidences, Lectures on Paley's Evidences, etc., 1 vol. Institutes of Theology, 2 vols. Political Economy : with Cognate Essays, 1 vol. Polity of a Nation, 1 vol. Church and College Establishments, 1 vol. Moral Philosophy, Introductory Essays, Index, etc., 1 vol.

Characteristics of Old Church Architecture, etc.,

In the Mainland and Western Islands of Scotland. 4to, with Illustrations, price 25s.

Dainty Dishes.

Receipts collected by LADY HARRIETT ST. CLAIR. New Edition, with many new Receipts. Crown 8vo. Price 5s.

"Well worth buying, especially by that class of persons who, though their incomes are small, enjoy out-of-the-way and recherché delicacies."—*Times.*

Ballads from Scottish History.

By NORVAL CLYNE. Fcap. 8vo, price 6s.

Sir John Duke Coleridge's

Inaugural Address at Edinburgh Philosophical Institution, Session 1870-71. 8vo, price 1s.

Wild Men and Wild Beasts—Adventures in Camp and

Jungle By LIEUT.-COLONEL GORDON CUMMING. Demy 8vo, with Illustrations by Lieut.-Col. BAIGRIE.

Notes on the Natural History of the Strait of Magellan
and West Coast of Patagonia, made during the voyage of H.M.S. 'Nassau' in the years 1866, 1867, 1868, and 1869. By ROBERT O. CUNNINGHAM, M.D., F.R.S., Naturalist to the Expedition. With Maps and numerous Illustrations. 8vo.

The Annals of the University of Edinburgh.
By ANDREW DALZEL, formerly Professor of Greek in the University of Edinburgh; with a Memoir of the Compiler, and Portrait after Raeburn. 2 vols. demy 8vo, price 21s.

Gisli the Outlaw.
From the Icelandic. By G. W. DASENT, D.C.L. Small 4to, with Illustrations, price 7s. 6d.

The Story of Burnt Njal;
Or, Life in Iceland at the end of the Tenth Century. From the Icelandic of the Njals Saga. By GEORGE WEBBE DASENT, D.C.L. 2 vols. 8vo, with Map and Plans, price 28s.

Select Popular Tales from the Norse.
For the use of Young People. By G. W. DASENT, D.C.L. New Edition, with Illustrations. Crown 8vo, 6s.

Plates and Notes relating to some Special Features in Structures called Pyramids. By ST. JOHN VINCENT DAY, C.E., F.R.SS.A. Royal folio, price 28s.

Papers on the Great Pyramid.
By ST. JOHN VINCENT DAY, C.E., F.R.SS.A. 8vo, price 4s.

The Law of Railways applicable to Scotland, with an
Appendix of Statutes and Forms. By FRANCIS DEAS, M.A., L.L.B., Advocate, Demy 8vo.

On the Application of Sulphurous Acid Gas
to the Prevention, Limitation, and Cure of Contagious Diseases. By JAMES DEWAR, M.D. Thirteenth edition, price 1s.

Memoir of Thomas Drummond, R.E., F.R.A.S., Under-Secretary to the Lord-Lieutenant of Ireland, 1835 to 1840. By JOHN F. M'LENNAN, Advocate. 8vo, price 15s.
"A clear, compact, and well-written memoir of the best friend England ever gave to Ireland."—*Examiner.*

A Political Survey.
By MOUNTSTUART E. GRANT DUFF, Member for the Elgin District of Burghs; Author of "Studies in European Politics," "A Glance over Europe," &c. &c. 8vo, price 7s. 6d.

"In following up his 'Studies in European Politics' by the 'Political Survey' here before us, Mr. Grant Duff has given strong evidence of the wisdom of the choice made by the Ministry in appointing him Under-Secretary for India. In the space of about 240 pages, he gives us the cream of the latest information about the internal politics of no less than forty-four different countries under four heads, according to their situation in Europe, Asia, and Africa, Northern and Central America, or South America."—*Pall Mall Gazette.*

By the same Author.

A Glance over Europe. Price 1s.

Inaugural Address to the University of Aberdeen, on his
Installation as Rector. Price 1s.

East India Financial Statement, 1869. Price 1s.

Remarks on the Present Political Situation.
A Speech delivered at Elgin, Nov. 15, 1870. Price 1s.

Veterinary Medicines; their Actions and Uses.
By FINLAY DUN. Third Edition, revised and enlarged. 8vo, price 12s.

Social Life in Former Days;
Chiefly in the Province of Moray. Illustrated by letters and family papers. By E. DUNBAR DUNBAR, late Captain 21st Fusiliers. 2 vols. demy 8vo, price 19s. 6d.

Deep-Sea Soundings.
COLLOQUIA PERIPATETICA. By the late JOHN DUNCAN, LL.D., Professor of Hebrew in the New College, Edinburgh; being Conversations in Philosophy, Theology, and Religion. Second Edition. 1 vol. fcap. 8vo. Price 3s. 6d.

"The present volume, if nothing more of Dr. Duncan's wonderful talk than what its pages contain were ever to emerge, would yet be an adequate monument to the deceased, and a gift of the highest value to our speculative literature."—*Daily Review.*

Karl's Legacy.
By the REV. J. W. EBSWORTH. 2 vols. ex. fcap. 8vo. Price 6s. 6d.

Charlie and Ernest; or, Play and Work.
A Story of Hazlehurst School, with Four Illustrations by J. D. By M. BETHAM EDWARDS. Royal 16mo, 3s. 6d.

A Memoir of the Right Honourable Hugh Elliot.
By his Granddaughter, the COUNTESS of MINTO. 8vo, price 12s.

"Lady Minto produced a valuable memoir when she printed the substance of the work before us for private circulation in 1862. It now, in its completed shape, presents a full length and striking portrait of a remarkable member of a remarkable race."—*Quarterly Review.*

The Unconditional Freeness of the Gospel.
New Edition revised. By the late THOMAS ERSKINE of Linlathen. 1 vol. fcap. 8vo. Price 3s. 6d.

By the same Author.

The Purpose of God in the Creation of Man.
Fcap. 8vo, sewed. Price 6d.

Good Little Hearts.
By AUNT FANNY. Author of the "Night-Cap Series." 4 vols. in a box, price 6s.

L'Histoire d'Angleterre. Par M. LAMÉ FLEURY. 18mo, cloth, 2s. 6d.

L'Histoire de France. Par M. LAMÉ FLEURY. 18mo, cloth, 2s. 6d.

Christianity viewed in some of its Leading Aspects.
By REV. A. L. R. FOOTE, Author of 'Incidents in the Life of our Saviour.' Fcap., cloth, 3s.

Kalendars of Scottish Saints, with Personal Notices of those
of Alba. By ALEXANDER PENROSE FORBES, D.C.L., Bishop of Brechin. 1 vol. 4to. Price to *Subscribers only*, Two Guineas. Large paper copies, Four Guineas.

Frost and Fire;
Natural Engines, Tool-Marks, and Chips, with Sketches drawn at Home and Abroad by a Traveller. Re-issue, containing an additional Chapter. 2 vols. 8vo, with Maps and numerous Illustrations on Wood, price 21s.

"A very Turner among books, in the originality and delicious freshness of its style, and the truth and delicacy of the descriptive portions. For some four-and-twenty years he has traversed half our northern hemisphere by the least frequented paths; and everywhere, with artistic and philosophic eye, has found something to describe—here in tiny trout-stream or fleecy cloud, there in lava-flow or ocean current, or in the works of nature's giant sculptor—ice."—*Reader.*

The Cat's Pilgrimage.
By J. A. FROUDE, M.A., late Fellow of Exeter College, Oxford. With 7 full-page Illustrations by Mrs. BLACKBURN (J. B.). 4to, price 6s.

Gifts for Men. By X. H.
1. The Gift of Repentance.
2. The Gift of the Yoke.
3. The Gift of the Holy Ghost.
4. The Promise to the Elect.

Crown 8vo, price 6

"Written in a very Christian spirit, and with much skill, originality, and fervour."—*Publisher's Circular.*

Arthurian Localities: their Historical Origin, Chief Country,
and Fingalian Relations, with a Map of Arthurian Scotland. By JOHN G. S. STUART GLENNIE, M.A. 8vo, price 7s. 6d.

Works by Margaret Maria Gordon (nee Brewster).
LADY ELINOR MORDAUNT; or, Sunbeams in the Castle. Crown 8vo, cloth, 9s.

WORK; or, Plenty to do and How to do it. Thirty-fifth thousand. Fcap. 8vo, cloth, 2s. 6d.

LITTLE MILLIE AND HER FOUR PLACES. Cheap Edition. Fifty-third thousand. Limp cloth, 1s.

SUNBEAMS IN THE COTTAGE; or, What Women may do. A narrative chiefly addressed to the Working Classes. Cheap Edition. Forty-third thousand. Limp cloth, 1s.

PREVENTION; or, An Appeal to Economy and Common-Sense. 8vo, 6d.

THE WORD AND THE WORLD. Price 2d.

LEAVES OF HEALING FOR THE SICK AND SORROWFUL. Fcap. 4to, cloth, 3s. 6d. Cheap Edition, limp cloth, 2s.

THE MOTHERLESS BOY; with an Illustration by J. NOEL PATON, R.S.A. Cheap Edition, limp cloth, 1s.

"Alike in manner and matter calculated to attract youthful attention, and to attract it by the best of all means—sympathy."—*Scotsman.*

'Christopher North;'

A Memoir of John Wilson, late Professor of Moral Philosophy in the University of Edinburgh. Compiled from Family Papers and other sources, by his daughter, MRS. GORDON. Third Thousand. 2 vols. crown 8vo, price 24s., with Portrait, and graphic Illustrations.

'Mystifications.'

By Miss STIRLING GRAHAM. Fourth Edition. Edited by JOHN BROWN, M.D. With Portrait of Lady Pitlyal. Fcap. 8vo., price 3s. 6d.

Life of Father Lacordaire.

By DORA GREENWELL. Fcap. 8vo. Price 6s.

"She has done a great service in bringing before the English public the career of a great man whose biography they might have refused to read if written by a Roman Catholic."—*Church Times.*

Scenes from the Life of Jesus.

By SAMUEL GREG. Second Edition, enlarged. Ex. fcap. 8vo, price 3s. 6d.

"One of the few theological works which can be heartily commended to all classes."—*Inverness Courier.*

Arboriculture; or A Practical Treatise on Raising and

Managing Forest Trees, and on the Profitable Extension of the Woods and Forests of Great Britain. By JOHN GRIGOR, The Nurseries, Forres. 8vo, price 10s. 6d.

"He is a writer whose authorship has this weighty recommendation, that he can support his theories by facts, and can point to lands, worth less than a shilling an acre when he found them, now covered with ornamental plantations, and yielding through them a revenue equal to that of the finest corn-land in the country. . . . His book has interest both for the adept and the novice, for the large proprietor and him that has but a nook or corner to plant out."—*Saturday Review.*

"Mr. Grigor's practical information on all points on which an intending planter is interested is particularly good. . . . We have placed it on our shelves as a first-class book of reference on all points relating to Arboriculture; and we strongly recommend others to do the same."—*Farmer.*

An Ecclesiastical History of Scotland,

From the Introduction of Christianity to the Present Time. By GEORGE GRUB, A.M. 4 vols. 8vo, 42s. Fine Paper Copies, 52s. 6d.

Chronicle of Gudrun;

A Story of the North Sea. From the mediæval German. By EMMA LETHER-BROW. With frontispiece by J. NOEL PATON, R.S.A. New Edition, price 5s.

Notes on the Early History of the Royal Scottish Academy

By Sir GEORGE HARVEY, Kt., P.R.S.A. 8vo, price 3s. 6d.

The Life of our Lord.

By the Rev. WILLIAM HANNA, D.D., LL.D. 6 vols., handsomely bound in cloth extra, gilt edges, price 30s.

Separate vols., plain cloth, price 5s. each.

1. THE EARLIER YEARS OF OUR LORD. 8th Thousand.
2. THE MINISTRY IN GALILEE. Second Edition.
3. THE CLOSE OF THE MINISTRY. 6th Thousand.
4. THE PASSION WEEK. 5th Thousand.
5. THE LAST DAY OF OUR LORD'S PASSION. 47th Thousand.
6. THE FORTY DAYS AFTER THE RESURRECTION. 9th Thousand.

Heavenly Love and Earthly Echoes.

By a Glasgow Merchant. 2d Edition. 18mo, price 1s. 6d.

"We have read this volume with unmingled satisfaction. We very cordially recommend it, as one much fitted to commend religion to the young, to cheer and help the tempted and desponding, and indeed to have a wholesome influence on the minds and hearts of all."—*Original Secession Magazine.*

Herminius.

A Romance. By I. E. S. Fcap. 8vo, price 6s.

The Historians of Scotland.

An Annual Payment of £1 will entitle the Subscriber to Two volumes. *Price to Non-Subscribers*, 15s. *per volume.*

In Preparation.

1. **Scoticronicon of John de Fordun, from a contemporary** MS. at the end of the Fourteenth century, preserved in the Library at Wolfenbüttel, in the Duchy of Brunswick; collated with other known MSS. of the original chronicle. Edited by Mr. WILLIAM F. SKENE. In 2 vols. demy 8vo.

2. **The Metrical Chronicle of Andrew of Wyntoun, Prior of** St. Serf's Inch in Lochleven, who died about 1426. The work now printed entire for the first time, from the Royal MS. in the British Museum, collated with other MSS. Edited by Mr. DAVID LAING. In demy 8vo.

If the Gospel Narratives are Mythical, what then?

Crown 8vo., price 3s. 6d.

"This intensely interesting treatise."—*The Watchman.*

"Many of the author's remarks are extremely beautiful and suggestive, the result of accurate and earnest thought."—*Freeman.*

Sketches of Early Scotch History.

By COSMO INNES, F.S.A., Professor of History in the University of Edinburgh. 1. The Church; its Old Organisation, Parochial and Monastic. 2. Universities. 3. Family History. 8vo, price 16s.

Concerning some Scotch Surnames.

By COSMO INNES, F.S.A., Professor of History in the University of Edinburgh. Small 4to, cloth antique, 5s.

Instructive Picture Books.

Folio, 7s. 6d. each.

"These Volumes are among the most instructive Picture-books we have seen, and we know of none better calculated to excite and gratify the appetite of the young for the knowledge of nature."—*Times.*

I.

The Instructive Picture Book. A few Attractive Lessons from the Natural History of Animals. By ADAM WHITE, late Assistant, Zoological Department, British Museum. With 54 folio coloured Plates. Seventh Edition, containing many new Illustrations by Mrs. BLACKBURN, J. STEWART, GOURLAY STEELL, and others.

II.

The Instructive Picture Book. Lessons from the Vegetable World. By the Author of 'The Heir of Redclyffe,' 'The Herb of the Field,' etc. Arranged by ROBERT M. STARK, Edinburgh. New Edition, with 64 Plates.

III.

Instructive Picture Book. The Geographical Distribution of Animals, in a Series of Pictures for the use of Schools and Families. By the late Dr. GREVILLE. With descriptive letterpress. New Edition, with 60 Plates.

IV.

Pictures of Animal and Vegetable Life in all Lands. 48 Folio Plates.

The History of Scottish Poetry,

From the Middle Ages to the Close of the Seventeenth Century. By the late DAVID IRVING, LL.D. Edited by JOHN AITKEN CARLYLE, M.D. With a Memoir and Glossary. Demy 8vo, 16s.

Sermons by the Rev. John Ker, D.D., Glasgow.

Eighth Edition. Crown 8vo, price 6s.

"This is a very remarkable volume of sermons. And it is no doubt a most favourable symptom of the healthiness of Christian thought among us, that we are so often able to begin a notice with these words.

"We cannot help wishing that such notice more frequently introduced to our readers a volume of Church of England sermons. Still, looking beyond our pale, we rejoice notwithstanding.

"Mr. Ker has dug boldly and diligently into the vein which Robertson opened; but the result, as compared with that of the first miner, is as the product of skilled machinery set against that of the vigorous unaided arm. There is no roughness, no sense of labour; all comes smoothly and regularly on the page—one thought evoked out of another. As Robertson strikes the rock with his tool, unlooked-for sparkles tempt him on; the workman exults in his discovery; behind each beautiful, strange thought, there is yet another more strange and beautiful still. Whereas, in this work, every beautiful thought has its way prepared, and every strange thought loses its power of starting by the exquisite harmony of its setting. Robertson's is the glitter of the ore on the bank; Ker's is the uniform shining of the wrought metal. We have not seen a volume of sermons for many a day which will so thoroughly repay both purchase and perusal and re-perusal. And not the least merit of these sermons is, that they are eminently suggestive."—*Contemporary Review.*

" The sermons before us are indeed of no common order ; among a host of competitors they occupy a high class—we were about to say the highest class—whether viewed in point of composition, or thought, or treatment.

" He has gone down in the diving-bell of a sound Christian philosophy, to the very depth of his theme, and has brought up treasures of the richest and most *recherché* character, practically showing the truth of his own remarks in the preface, ' that there is no department of thought or action which cannot be touched by that gospel which is the manifold wisdom of God.' These subjects he has exhibited in a style corresponding to their brilliancy and profoundness — terse and telling, elegant and captivating, yet totally unlike the tinsel ornaments laid upon the subject by an elaborate process of manipulation—a style which is the outcome of the sentiment and feelings within, shaping itself in appropriate drapery."—*British and Foreign Evangelical Review.*

Readings in Holy Writ.
By LORD KINLOCH. Fcap. 8vo.

Faith's Jewels.
Presented in Verse, with other devout Verses. By LORD KINLOCH. Ex. fcap. 8vo, price 5s.

The Circle of Christian Doctrine ;
A Handbook of Faith, framed out of a Layman's experience. By LORD KINLOCH. Third and Cheaper Edition. Fcap. 8vo, 2s. 6d.

Time's Treasure ;
Or, Devout Thoughts for every Day of the Year. Expressed in verse. By LORD KINLOCH. Third and Cheaper Edition. Fcap. 8vo, price 3s. 6d.

Devout Moments.
By LORD KINLOCH. Price 6d.

Studies for Sunday Evening.
By LORD KINLOCH. Second Edition. Fcap. 8vo, price 4s. 6d.

Supplemental Descriptive Catalogue of Ancient Scottish Seals.
By HENRY LAING. 4to, profusely illustrated, price £3 : 3s.

The Philosophy of Ethics :
An Analytical Essay. By SIMON S. LAURIE, A.M. Demy 8vo, price 6s.

Notes, Expository and Critical, on certain British Theories
of Morals. By SIMON S. LAURIE. 8vo, price 6s.

The Reform of the Church of Scotland
In Worship, Government, and Doctrine. By ROBERT LEE, D.D., late Professor of Biblical Criticism in the University of Edinburgh, and Minister of Greyfriars. Part I. Worship. Second Edition, fcap. 8vo, price 3s.

Historical Records of the Family of Leslie.
From A.D. 1067 to 1868-69. Collected from Public Records and Authentic Private Sources. By Colonel CHARLES LESLIE, K.H., of Balquhain. 3 vols. demy 8vo, price 36s.

Life in Normandy;

Sketches of French Fishing, Farming, Cooking, Natural History, and Politics, drawn from Nature. By an ENGLISH RESIDENT. Third Edition, crown 8vo, price 6s.

A Memoir of Lady Anna Mackenzie,

Countess of Balcarres, and afterwards of Argyle, 1621-1706. By ALEXANDER LORD LINDSAY. Fcap. 8vo, price 3s. 6d.

" All who love the byways of history, should read this life of a loyal covenanter."
—*Atlas.*

Little Ella and the Fire-King,

And other Fairy Tales. By M. W., with Illustrations by HENRY WARREN. Second Edition. 16mo, cloth, 3s. 6d.   Cloth extra, gilt edges, 4s.

Primary and Classical Education.

By the Right Hon. ROBERT LOWE, M.P.   Price 1s.

Specimens of Ancient Gaelic Poetry.

Collected between the years 1512 and 1529 by the REV. JAMES M'GREGOR, Dean of Lismore—illustrative of the Language and Literature of the Scottish Highlands prior to the Sixteenth Century.   Edited, with a Translation and Notes, by the Rev. THOMAS MACLAUCHLAN. The Introduction and additional Notes by WILLIAM F. SKENE. 8vo, price 12s.

Ten Years North of the Orange River.

A Story of Everyday Life and Work among the South African Tribes, from 1859 to 1869.   By JOHN MACKENZIE, of the London Missionary Society.   With Map and Illustrations. 1 vol. crown 8vo, price 6s.

Select Writings: Political, Scientific, Topographical, and

Miscellaneous, of the late CHARLES MACLAREN, F.R.S.E., F.G.S., Editor of the *Scotsman.* Edited by ROBERT COX, F.S.A., Scot., and JAMES NICOL, F.R.S.E., F.G.S., Professor of Natural History in the University of Aberdeen.   With a Memoir and Portrait. 2 vols. crown 8vo, 15s.

Memorials of the Life and Ministry of Charles Calder

Mackintosh, D.D. of Tain and Dunoon.   Edited, with a Sketch of the Religious History of the Northern Highlands of Scotland, by the Rev. WILLIAM TAYLOR, M.A., with Portrait. Crown 8vo, price 6s.

The Americans at Home.

Pen and Ink Sketches of American Men, Manners, and Institutions. By DAVID MACRAE. 2 vols. crown 8vo., price 16s.

" A really good work on America, which deserves to be cordially welcomed. It is replete with racy and original anecdotes, and abounds with realistic pictures of American life and character."—*Westminster Review.*

Macvicar's (J. G., D.D.)

THE PHILOSOPHY OF THE BEAUTIFUL; price 6s. 6d.   FIRST LINES OF SCIENCE SIMPLIFIED; price 5s.   INQUIRY INTO HUMAN NATURE; price 7s. 6d.

Mary Stuart and the Casket Letters.
By J. F. N., with an Introduction by HENRY GLASSFORD BELL. Ex. fcap. 8vo, price 4s. 6d.

Max Havalaar;
Or, The Coffee Auctions of the Dutch Trading Company. By MULTATULI; translated from the original MS. by Baron Nahuys. With Maps, price 14s.

Why the Shoe Pinches.
A contribution to Applied Anatomy. By HERMANN MEYER, M.D., Professor of Anatomy in the University of Zurich. Price 6d.

The Herring:
Its Natural History and National Importance. By JOHN M. MITCHELL. With Six Illustrations, 8vo, price 12s.

The Insane in Private Dwellings.
By ARTHUR MITCHELL, A.M., M.D., Deputy Commissioner in Lunacy for Scotland, etc. 8vo, price 4s. 6d.

Creeds and Churches.
By the REV. SIR HENRY WELLWOOD MONCREIFF, Bart., D.D. Demy 8vo. Price 3s. 6d.

Ancient Pillar-Stones of Scotland:
Their Significance and Bearing on Ethnology. By GEORGE MOORE, M.D. 8vo, price 6s. 6d.

Heroes of Discovery.
By SAMUEL MOSSMAN. Crown 8vo, price 5s.

Political Sketches of the State of Europe—from 1814-1867.
Containing Ernest, Count Münster's Despatches to the Prince Regent from the Congress of Vienna and of Paris. By GEORGE HERBERT, Count Münster. Demy 8vo, price 9s.

Biographical Annals of the Parish of Colinton.
By THOMAS MURRAY, LL.D. Crown 8vo, price 3s. 6d.

History Rescued, in Answer to "History Vindicated," being
a recapitulation of "The Case for the Crown," and the Reviewers Reviewed, in re the Wigtown Martyrs. By MARK NAPIER. 8vo, price 5s.

Nightcaps:
A Series of Juvenile Books. By "AUNT FANNY." 6 vols. square 16mo, cloth. In case, price 12s., or separately, 2s. each volume.
1. Baby Nightcaps.   3. Big Nightcaps.   5. Old Nightcaps.
2. Little Nightcaps.   4. New Nightcaps.   6. Fairy Nightcaps.

"Neither a single story nor a batch of tales in a single volume, but a box of six pretty little books of choice fiction is Aunt Fanny's contribution to the new supply of literary toys for the next children's season. Imagine the delight of a little girl who, through the munificence of mamma or godmamma, finds herself possessor of Aunt Fanny's tastefully-decorated box. Conceive the exultation with which, on raising the lid, she discovers that it contains six whole and separate volumes, and then say, you grown-up folk, whose pockets are bursting with florins, whether you do not think that a few of your pieces of white money would be well laid out in purchasing such pleasure for the tiny damsels of your acquaintance, who like to be sent to bed with the fancies of a pleasant story-teller clothing their sleepy heads with nightcaps of dreamy contentment. The only objection we can make to the quality and fashion of Aunt Fanny's Nightcaps is, that some of their joyous notions are more calculated to keep infantile wearers awake all night than to dispose them to slumber. As nightcaps for the daytime, however, they are, one and all, excellent."—*Athenæum.*

ODDS AND ENDS—*Price 6d. Each.*

Vol. I., in Cloth, price 4s. 6d., containing Nos. 1-10.
Vol. II., Do. do. Nos. 11-19.

1. Sketches of Highland Character.
2. Convicts.
3. Wayside Thoughts.
4. The Enterkin.
5. Wayside Thoughts—Part 2.
6. Penitentiaries and Reformatories.
7. Notes from Paris.
8. Essays by an Old Man.
9. Wayside Thoughts—Part 3.
10. The Influence of the Reformation.
11. The Cattle Plague.
12. Rough Night's Quarters.
13. On the Education of Children.
14. The Stormontfield Experiments.
15. A Tract for the Times.
16. Spain in 1866.
17. The Highland Shepherd.
18. Correlation of Forces.
19. 'Bibliomania.'
20. A Tract on Twigs.
21. Notes on Old Edinburgh.
22. Gold-Diggings in Sutherland.
23. Post-Office Telegraphs.

The Bishop's Walk and The Bishop's Times.
By ORWELL. Fcap. 8vo, price 5s.

Man: Where, Whence, and Whither?
Being a glance at Man in his Natural-History Relations. By DAVID PAGE, LL.D. Fcap. 8vo, price 3s. 6d.
"Cautiously and temperately written."—*Spectator.*

The Great Sulphur Cure.
By ROBERT PAIRMAN, Surgeon. Thirteenth Edition, price 1s.

France: Two Lectures.
By M. PREVOST-PARADOL, of the French Academy. 8vo, price 2s. 6d.
"Should be carefully studied by every one who wishes to know anything about contemporary French History."—*Daily Review.*

Suggestions on Academical Organisation,
With Special Reference to Oxford. By MARK PATTISON, B.D., Rector of Lincoln College, Oxford. Crown 8vo, price 7s. 6d.

Practical Water-Farming.
By WM. PEARD, M.D., LL.D. 1 vol. fcap. 8vo, price 5s.

Memoirs of Frederick Perthes ;
Or, Literary, Religious, and Political Life in Germany from 1789 to 1848. By C. T. PERTHES, Professor of Law at Bonn. Crown 8vo, cloth, 6s.

On Primary and Technical Education.
Two Lectures delivered to the Philosophical Institution of Edinburgh. By LYON PLAYFAIR, C.B., M.P. 8vo., price 1s.

Popular Genealogists ;
Or, The Art of Pedigree-making. Crown 8vo, price 4s.

The Pyramid and the Bible:
The rectitude of the one in accordance with the truth of the other. By a CLERGY-MAN. Ex. fcap. 8vo, price 3s. 6d.

Reminiscences of Scottish Life and Character.
By E. B. RAMSAY, M.A., LL.D., F.R.S.E., Dean of Edinburgh. Nineteenth Edition, price 1s. 6d.

" The Dean of Edinburgh has here produced a book for railway reading of the very first class. The persons (and they are many) who can only under such circumstances devote ten minutes of attention to any page, without the certainty of a dizzy or stupid headache, in every page of this volume will find some poignant anecdote or trait which will last them a good half-hour for after-laughter: one of the pleasantest of human sensations."—*Athenæum.*

„ The original Edition in 2 vols. with Introductions, price 12s., and the Sixteenth Edition in 1 vol. cloth antique, price 6s., may be had.

Recess Studies.
Edited by Sir ALEXANDER GRANT, Bart., LL.D. 8vo, price 12s.

Art Rambles in Shetland.
By JOHN T. REID. Handsome 4to, cloth, profusely Illustrated, price 25s.

" This record of Art Rambles may be classed among the most choice and highly-finished of recent publications of this sort."—*Saturday Review.*

Historical Studies.
By E. WILLIAM ROBERTSON, Author of " Scotland under her Early Kings."

CONTENTS.

1. STANDARDS OF THE PAST.	4. THE KING'S KIN.
2. LAND.	5. THE CORONATION OF EDGAR.
3. THE KING'S WIFE.	6. THE POLICY OF DUNSTAN.

ETC. ETC. ETC. In 1 vol. Demy 8vo.

Scotland under her Early Kings.
A History of the Kingdom to the close of the 13th century. By E. WILLIAM ROBERTSON, in 2 vols. 8vo, cloth, 36s.

Doctor Antonio.

A Tale. By JOHN RUFFINI. Cheap Edition, crown 8vo, boards, 2s. 6d.

Lorenzo Benoni ;

Or, Passages in the Life of an Italian. By JOHN RUFFINI. With Illustrations. Crown 8vo, cloth gilt, 5s. Cheap Edition, crown 8vo, boards, 2s. 6d.

The Salmon ;

Its History, Position, and Prospects. By ALEX. RUSSEL.' 8vo, price 7s. 6d.

Druidism Exhumed. Proving that the Stone Circles of

Britain were Druidical Temples. By Rev. JAMES RUST. Fcap. 8vo, price 4s. 6d.

Gowodean :

A Pastoral, by JAMES SALMON. 8vo, price 6s.

Natural History and Sport in Moray.

Collected from the Journals and Letters of the late CHARLES St. JOHN, Author of 'Wild Sports of the Highlands.' With a short Memoir of the Author. Crown 8vo, price 8s. 6d.

A Handbook of the History of Philosophy.

By Dr. ALBERT SCHWEGLER. Second Edition. Translated and Annotated by J. HUTCHISON STIRLING, LL.D., Author of the 'Secret of Hegel.' Crown 8vo, price 6s.

"Schwegler's is the best possible handbook of the history of philosophy, and there could not possibly be a better translator of it than Dr. Stirling."—*Westminster Review.*

The Scottish Poor-Laws : Examination of their Policy,

History, and Practical Action. By SCOTUS. 8vo, price 7s. 6d.

"This book is a magazine of interesting facts and acute observations upon this vitally important subject."—*Scotsman.*

The Roman Poets of the Republic.

By W. Y. SELLAR, M.A., Professor of Humanity in the University of Edinburgh, and formerly Fellow of Oriel College, Oxford. 8vo, price 12s.

Gossip about Letters and Letter-Writers.

By GEORGE SETON, Advocate, M.A., Oxon., F.S.A., Scot. Fcap. 8vo, price 5s.

"A very agreeable little *brochure* which anybody may dip into with satisfaction to while away idle hours."—*Echo.*

'Cakes, Leeks, Puddings, and Potatoes.'

A Lecture on the Nationalities of the United Kingdom. By GEORGE SETON, Advocate, M.A., Oxon, etc. Second Edition. Fcap. 8vo, sewed, price 6d.

Culture and Religion.

By J. C. SHAIRP, Principal of the United College of St. Salvator and St. Leonards, St. Andrews. Fcap. 8vo, price 3s. 6d.

"A wise book, and unlike a great many other wise books, has that carefully-shaded thought and expression which fits Professor Shairp to speak for Culture no less than for Religion."—*Spectator.*

John Keble:

An Essay on the Author of the 'Christian Year.' By J. C. SHAIRP, Principal of the United College of St. Salvator and St. Leonards, St. Andrews. Fcap. 8vo, price 3s.

"It is difficult to praise such a book as it deserves without seeming to exaggerate, and still more difficult to give the reader any fair idea of its beauty and power by mere quotation."—*Watchman.*

"The finest essay in this volume, partly because it is upon the greatest and most definite subject, is the first—Wordsworth. . . We have said so much upon this essay that we can only say of the three others, that they are fully worthy to stand beside it."—*Spectator.*

Studies in Poetry and Philosophy.

By J. C. SHAIRP, St. Andrews. 1 vol. fcap. 8vo, price 6s.

On Archaic Sculpturings of Cups and Circles upon Stones

and Rocks in Scotland, England, etc. By Sir J. Y. SIMPSON, Bart., M.D., D.C.L., Vice-President of the Society of Antiquaries of Scotland, etc. etc. 1 vol. small 4to, with Illustrations, price 21s.

Proposal to Stamp out Small-pox and other Contagious

Diseases. By Sir J. Y. SIMPSON, Bart., M.D., D.C.L. Price 1s.

The Four Ancient Books of Wales,

Containing the Cymric Poems attributed to the Bards of the Sixth century.' By WILLIAM F. SKENE. With Maps and Facsimiles. 2 vols. 8vo, price 36s.

"Mr. Skene's book will, as a matter of course and necessity, find its place on the tables of all Celtic antiquarians and scholars."—*Archæologia Cambrensis.*

The Coronation Stone.

By WILLIAM F. SKENE. Small 4to. With Illustrations in Photography and Zincography. Price 6s.

The Sermon on the Mount.

By the Rev. WALTER C. SMITH, Author of 'The Bishop's Walk, and other Poems, by Orwell,' and 'Hymns of Christ and Christian Life.' Crown 8vo, price 6s.

Disinfectants and Disinfection.

By Dr. ROBERT ANGUS SMITH. 8vo, price 5s.

"By common consent Dr. Angus Smith has become the first authority in Europe on the subject of Disinfectants. To this subject he has devoted a large portion of his scientific life; and now, in a compact volume of only 138 pages, he has condensed the result of twenty years of patient study. To Sanitary officers, to municipal and parochial authorities, and, indeed, to all who are particularly concerned for the public health and life; and who is not? we sincerely commend Dr. Angus Smith's treatise."—*Chemical News.*

Life and Work at the Great Pyramid.

With a Discussion of the Facts Ascertained. By C. PIAZZI SMYTH, F.R.SS.L. and E., Astronomer-Royal for Scotland. 3 vols. demy 8vo, price 56s.

On the Antiquity of Intellectual Man from a Practical and

Astronomical Point of View. By C. PIAZZI SMYTH, F.R.SS.L. and E., Astronomer-Royal for Scotland. Crown 8vo, price 9s.

An Equal-Surface Projection for Maps of the World, and
its Application to certain Anthropological Questions. By C. PIAZZI SMYTH,
F.R.SS.L. & E., Astronomer-Royal for Scotland. 8vo, price 3s.

History Vindicated in the Case of the Wigtown Martyrs.
By the Rev. ARCHIBALD STEWART. Second Edition. 8vo, price 3s. 6d.

Dugald Stewart's Collected Works.
Edited by Sir WILLIAM HAMILTON, Bart. Vols. I. to X. 8vo, cloth, each 12s.
Vol. I.—Dissertation. Vols. II. III. and IV.—Elements of the Philosophy
of the Human Mind. Vol. V.—Philosophical Essays. Vols. VI. and VII.—
Philosophy of the Active and Moral Powers of Man. Vols. VIII. and IX.—
Lectures on Political Economy. Vol. X.—Biographical Memoirs of Adam
Smith, LL.D., William Robertson, D.D., and Thomas Reid, D.D.; to which
is prefixed a Memoir of Dugald Stewart, with Selections from his Corre-
spondence, by John Veitch, M.A. Supplementary Vol.—Translations of the
Passages in Foreign Languages contained in the Collected Works; with
General Index.

Jerrold, Tennyson, Macaulay, and other Critical Essays.
By JAMES HUTCHISON STIRLING, LL.D., Author of 'The Secret of Hegel.'
1 vol. fcap. 8vo, price 5s.

"The author of 'The Secret of Hegel' here gives us his opinions of the lives
and works of those three great representative Englishmen whose names appear on
the title-page of the work before us. Dr. Stirling's opinions are entitled to be heard,
and carry great weight with them. He is a lucid and agreeable writer, a profound
metaphysician, and by his able translations from the German has proved his grasp
of mind and wide acquaintance with philosophical speculation."—*Examiner.*

Christ the Consoler;
Or Scriptures, Hymns, and Prayers for Times of Trouble and Sorrow. Selected and
arranged by the Rev. ROBERT HERBERT STORY, Minister of Roseneath. Fcap. 8vo,
price 3s. 6d.

Outlines of Scottish Archæology.
By Rev. G. SUTHERLAND. 12mo, sewed, profusely Illustrated, price 1s.

Works by Professor James Syme.
OBSERVATIONS IN CLINICAL SURGERY. Second Edition. 8vo, price 8s. 6d.
STRICTURE OF THE URETHRA, AND FISTULA IN PERINEO. 8vo, 4s. 6d.
TREATISE ON THE EXCISION OF DISEASED JOINTS. 8vo, 5s.
ON DISEASES OF THE RECTUM. 8vo, 4s. 6d.
EXCISION OF THE SCAPULA. 8vo, price 2s. 6d.

Lessons for School Life.
Sermons preached in the Chapel of Rugby School. By HIS GRACE THE ARCH-
BISHOP OF CANTERBURY. Fcap. cloth, 5s.

Thermodynamics.
By P. G. TAIT, Professor of Natural Philosophy in the University of Edinburgh.
1 vol. 8vo, price 5s.

Day-Dreams of a Schoolmaster.
By D'ARCY W. THOMPSON. Second Edition. Fcap. 8vo, price 5s.

Sales Attici :
Or, The Maxims, Witty and Wise, of Athenian Tragic Drama. By D'ARCY WENT-
WORTH THOMPSON, Professor of Greek in Queen's College, Galway. Fcap. 8vo,
price 9s.

Memoir and Correspondence of Mr. Thomson of Banchory.
Edited by Professor SMEATON. Demy 8vo, price 9s.

From Pesth to Brindisi; being Notes of a Tour in the
Autumn of 1869 from Pesth to Belgrade, Constantinople, Athens, Corfu, Brindisi,
and Naples. By Sir CHARLES TREVELYAN. 8vo, sewed, price 1s.

Twelve Years in China :
By a British Resident. With coloured Illustrations. Second Edition. Crown
8vo, cloth, price 10s. 6d.

Travels by Umbra.
8vo., price 10s. 6d.

Hotch-Pot.
By UMBRA. An Old Dish with New Materials. Fcap. 8vo, price 3s. 6d.

The Merchant's Sermon and other Stories.
By L. B. WALFORD. 18mo, price 1s. 6d.

Memoirs of Alexandra, late Empress of Russia, and Wife of
Nicholas I. By M. DE GRIMM. Translated by LADY WALLACE. 2 vols. crown
8vo., price 21s.

Tiny Tales for Little Tots.
With Six Illustrations by WARWICK BROOKES. Square 18mo, price 1s.

What is Sabbath-Breaking ?
8vo, price 2s.

Dante's—The Inferno.
Translated line for line by W. P. WILKIE, Advocate. Fcap. 8vo, price 5s.

Life of Dr. John Reid,
Late Chandos Professor of Anatomy and Medicine in the University of St. Andrews.
By the late GEORGE WILSON, M.D. Fcap. 8vo, cloth, price 3s.

Researches on Colour-Blindness.
With a Supplement on the danger attending the present system of Railway and
Marine Coloured Signals. By the late GEORGE WILSON, M.D. 8vo, 5s.

An Historical Sketch of the French Bar from its Origin to
the Present Day. By ARCHIBALD YOUNG, Advocate. Demy 8vo. Price
7s. 6d.
"A useful contribution to our knowledge of the leading French politicians of
the present day."—*Saturday Review.*